1/03

PATENTLY
FEMALE

PATENTLY FEMALE

*From AZT to TV Dinners,
Stories of Women Inventors and
Their Breakthrough Ideas*

Ethlie Ann Vare

Greg Ptacek

JOHN WILEY & SONS, INC.

Copyright © 2002 by Ethlie Ann Vare and Greg Ptacek. All rights reserved
Foreword © copyright 2002 by Ruth Handler
Preface © copyright 2002 by Janet L. Rideout, Ph.D.
"Supercomputer and Microelectronics Chip Design" on pages 72–82 © copyright 2001 by
    Christina Soletti
"Genius in the Shadows: The Women of ENIAC" on pages 84–87 © copyright 1999 by Andy
    Tiemann

Published by John Wiley & Sons, Inc., New York
Published simultaneously in Canada

Design and production by Navta Associates, Inc.

This publication is designed to provide accurate and authoritative information in regard to
the subject matter covered. It is sold with the understanding that the publisher is not engaged
in rendering professional services. If professional advice or other expert assistance is
required, the services of a competent professional person should be sought.

Designations used by companies to distinguish their products are often claimed as trademarks. In all instances where John Wiley & Sons, Inc., is aware of a claim, the product names
appear in Initial Capital or ALL CAPITAL letters. Readers, however, should contact the
appropriate companies for more complete information regarding trademarks and registration.

Library of Congress Cataloging-in-Publication Data:

Vare, Ethlie Ann.
    Patently female : from AZT to TV dinners : stories of women inventors and their
breakthrough ideas / Ethlie Ann Vare and Greg Ptacek.
        p. cm.
    Continues: Mothers of invention.
    Includes bibliographical references and index.
    ISBN: 0-471-02334-5 (cloth : alk. paper)
        1. Women inventors. 2. Women inventors—United States—Biography. I. Ptacek, Greg.
II. Vare, Ethlie Ann. Mothers of invention. III. Title.

T36 .V38   2001
609.2'273—dc21
[B]   2001026950

CONTENTS

Foreword by Ruth Handler,
  inventor of the Barbie Doll   vii

Preface by Janet L. Rideout, Ph.D.,
  patented the AIDS-fighting drug AZT   ix

Acknowledgments   xiii

Introduction   1

CHAPTER 1   Practicalities   5

CHAPTER 2   "Woman's Work"   37

CHAPTER 3   Computer Liberation   59

CHAPTER 4   Medicine   89

CHAPTER 5   Mother Earth   115

CHAPTER 6   It Took a Woman   133

CHAPTER 7   Women in Space   151

CHAPTER 8   Fun and Games   169

CHAPTER 9   The Littlest Inventors   177

CHAPTER 10   Pathfinders and Forerunners   189

Timeline: A More Complete
  Chronology of Invention   197

APPENDIX A   Joining the Ranks . . .   201

APPENDIX B   Resources   205

Index   209

FOREWORD

You don't have to be an engineer or a mathematician or a scientist to be an inventor. To be an inventor you have to have certain creative talents: the talent to observe and the talent to conceive of a new idea. You have to be able to see a need, and you have to have a specific, concrete understanding of how to fill that need.

You can hire technicians and manufacturers to bring your idea to fruition. You don't have to know what materials will be used or what the manufacturing process will be. But you cannot go to these people and say to them, "Let's do this better." You have to know exactly what you want.

My first successful creations, Barbie and Ken, came from observing my own daughter playing with paper dolls. She always chose grown-up dolls, and I realized she was using the doll to project her own dreams of her future. I was convinced that if I could turn this play pattern with paper dolls into a three-dimensional doll, I could fill a very real need in the lives of little girls.

My next noteworthy creation was the Nearly Me breast prosthesis. This came from my personal experience of having to wear an artificial breast after my mastectomy. I was determined to design and market a totally new type of artificial breast, one that looked and felt natural and was sold by clerks who were trained to be sensitive and helpful.

With all my creations I have observed a need—a big, fat hole in the market—and insisted that my product be better than anything else in its field. And in all cases the characteristic of the product had to be completely and carefully defined by the creator, the person with the idea.

I don't personally hold a patent on Barbie, but I am the inventor of the Barbie doll. Not everybody can be an inventor or a designer or a creator. You have to be blessed with certain talents—and you have to use them.

—Ruth Handler

PREFACE

There is a certain kind of person, a person who likes mysteries, crossword puzzles . . . and baking. Who enjoys designing things, building things, and also sewing . . . who likes drawing, painting, playing a musical instrument. A person who likes quiet time and likes to listen but also looks forward to a lively debate. We have a name for that person: we call her a scientist.

No, science may not be fashionable. It may not seem glamorous. But it is all around us every day, and it makes our lives wonderful.

I was first drawn to science because it was logical. When I saw an educational film in high school that described water purification and sewage treatment (ugh!), I was impressed that it could be useful, as well. As a college freshman I chose five core courses because I thought each might be my major. I stuck with chemistry because I enjoyed working hard to figure things out. It wasn't always fun, but I liked the challenge. (It also is worth mentioning that a few Cs and Ds indicated less than a stellar career if I chose some of the other potential majors!)

My father always expected that if he paid my costs (minus what I earned in the summer) I would major in a useful subject, since one needed to earn a living. He didn't expect that I would get a master's degree, much less a Ph.D. But he appreciated that I was able to pay my way, and my high school instructor assured him that I could always teach.

Dad was a wise man who taught me anything I wanted to learn: pitching, throwing, catching, and batting a baseball; passing and drop-kicking a football; boxing. My grandmother ran the family lumber business, and she saw to it that I had a chance to learn to swim, ride horses, and play tennis. She was my mentor and companion in my formative years. I saw that a woman could do whatever she wanted if she was prepared to do it.

My grandmother taught me such lessons as "If you want jelly, pick berries" and "If you take the pay in advance, the job is much more tedious." She also marveled that she had seen technology progress from the horse and buggy to the automobile, airplanes, and space exploration and men on the moon. She wondered what else would happen. My mother taught me that an education was something to be valued and that life was fun.

I don't think of myself as an inventor. I don't make gadgets. I'm a chemist and drug researcher who knows the value of patenting one's discoveries when there is some indication of a biological activity associated with a desired therapeutic effect. I also know that you do this before the discoveries are of proven value. I learned this lesson from Dr. Trudy Elion. [For more on Gertrude Elion, see pages 91–93.]

A person who wants to discover and develop drugs needs to be able to withstand terrific highs and lows. With luck, you will enjoy some successes. But there is also frustration: only one out of ten thousand compounds has a chance of becoming a drug. The challenge is to stay fascinated by the science itself, to continue to learn new things throughout your career. By interacting with my colleagues I was able to learn the basics of biochemistry, pharmacology, toxicology, enzymology, immunology, virology, microbiology, and molecular biology. All of these enter into fine-tuning the potency, selectivity, toxic liability, and bioavalability of the chemical that will ultimately become a medicine prescribed by doctors.

It was fascinating and exciting to be part of the meteoric rise of 509U81—otherwise known as Compound S, or AZT. We all operated at warp speed making sure deadlines were met and that the people needed to perform next were ready to do their part. People really burned out! I was very nervous when it was time to administer the drug to people for the first time. It was extremely scary to think that you might hurt the people you want to help. When the compound went to market, all of us were proud and thrilled. The negative reception the drug received from some AIDS groups, along with the later court battles, made me and others of the inventors wonder how trying your darnedest to help people could be so misconstrued.

I still follow the press on HIV and worry that the disease is not yet conquered. But now I'm busy learning new science and having fun in a small company where everything you do has a visible effect. Inspire

Pharmaceuticals has the extraordinary record of having one issued U.S. patent and two Notices of Allowance since being established in the spring of 1995.

Like my grandmother, I can't wait to see what's going to happen next.

—Janet L. Rideout, Ph.D.

ACKNOWLEDGMENTS

Thanks to computer technology (much of it invented by women, of course), formatting, illustrating, and printing a book is faster and easier than ever.

Getting it written, unfortunately, is just as hard as it's always been.

We would like to thank the shipload of people it took to get this cruise to its destination.

First, thanks to our agent, Madeleine Morel, who underneath it all has always believed in us. Thanks to our publisher, John Wiley, and our editor, Stephen S. Power, for welcoming us into the family. Thanks to our attorney, Chuck Hurewitz, for making it a happy marriage.

Now for the big list. Researching a subject that history has conspired to ignore is one daunting task. An enormous number of generous and learned people led us to the information in this manuscript. Thank you to:

Paula Koop and Ruth Nyblod at the U.S. Patent and Trademark Office; Elaine Murakami at the U.S Department of Transportation; NASA; Fred Strohl of Oak Ridge National Laboratory; the National Women's Hall of Fame; the Intellectual Property Owners Foundation; the National Inventors Hall of Fame; Bill Doan and Peter Johnsen at the U.S. Department of Agriculture; Joanne Rhyes Davies and Julia Schopick at *Inventor's Digest* magazine; documentarians Sky Winslow, Kathryn Kleiman, and Annie Wood; computer historian Denise Gurer; historians W. Barkley Fritz, Lee Saegesser, and Francis Karnes; the Jet Propulsion Laboratory; K. C. Coles at the *Los Angeles Times* and Tim Petzinger at the *Wall Street Journal*; Alan Trantner of the Inventors Workshop; Maxine Smith, patent attorney; Carol Oldenburg at the Inventors Association of America; Bob Huehn at the Canadian Industrial Innovation Center; Joan Ferry of the Woodson Research Center; Janet Ruff at the Goddard Center; Georgeanne Carter, Michael Elliot, and Michael Williams of the *IEEE* journal; the Lemelson Center; the Mechanical Engineering Department of Kettering University; Planned Parenthood; the Bryan Lang Historical Library; Eric Crossley at

Duracell; Fran Lockwood at Valvoline; Marian Weiss at Union Carbide; Barb Gabriel at Bissell; Elizabeth King at Johnson & Johnson; Jackie Peterson at Pillsbury; Becky Haglund of Kraft Foods; Kimberly Monroe and Michael Thompson of John Wiley; Christina Soletti; Maile Speetjens; and the fifty or sixty others we're forgetting.

A major shout out to Bob and the gang at the Samuel Goldwyn Library in Hollywood.

A huge bouquet to Professor Fred Amram at the University of Minnesota, without whose expertise, willingness, and photo collection this book would not have been half as good.

We cannot find words to thank our research assistants: Kimberly Ball, who got the—forgive us—ball rolling; Andy Tiemann, who broke the back of the beast, frequently going far above and beyond the call of duty; and Darolyn Striley, who stuck around to find those last few, impossible facts.

Most of all, we want to thank all the women—inventors, entrepreneurs, scientists, discoverers—who patiently allowed themselves to be interviewed and, worse, photographed for this book. They, and the women who came before them, are the reason for all of this. We are forever in their debt.

PATENTLY FEMALE

INTRODUCTION

This volume serves, informally, as a sequel to the 1988 book *Mothers of Invention: From the Bra to the Bomb, Forgotten Women and Their Unforgettable Ideas*. In that collection, we tried to resurrect from the cracks of history the names and stories of remarkable women who changed the world—and were promptly ignored by it. Because while it's difficult for most people to name a woman inventor, that isn't for any lack of women inventors. It's for lack of press.

Of the first hundred patents ever issued in the industrialized world, one was to a woman: in 1635 Sarah Jerom received British Patent #87 for a machine that sliced timber. In 1715 American colonist Sybilla Masters received English Patent #401 for her corn mill. (Actually the paperwork was made out to Thomas Masters, for "a new Invencon found out by Sybilla, his wife.") The United States itself awarded its first patent to a woman in 1793, when Hannah Slater perfected her cotton sewing thread.

As far back as 1899, in a manual published by the U.S. Patent Office, one Fred Dieterich wrote, "That woman is rapidly coming to the front as an inventor is evidenced by the large increase in the number of patents being filed by them." Dieterich added, "It is an erroneous impression that women [merely] invent improvements on articles intended for their sex . . . they are constantly exercising their ingenuity in the direction of improving many devices which men only as a rule are supposed to."

He mentions some women inventors and even goes so far as to say, "As a rule, inventions the product of the fair sex [are] not the extreme chimerical or visionary kind too often the product of the inexperienced 'first time' male."

In other words, women's inventions are prevalent, they are practical, and they are profitable. Somehow, though, this information is the victim of a strange historical amnesia. Almost a century later, when we researched *Mothers of Invention*, we discovered to our dismay that there were no books about women inventors on the shelves. Nor were there any mentions of women inventors in books written about inventors in general. The closest we came in our research was a chapter in the 1957 book *Inventors and Invention* by then–RCA patent director C. D. Tuska. The chapter was called "Age and Sex of Inventors."

"There are few women inventors," wrote Tuska. "I shall write little about the female inventors and, with natural caution, nothing about their ages. Most of our inventors are of the male sex. Why is the percentage of women so low? I'm sure I do not know, except the good Lord intended them to be mothers. They produce the inventors and help rear them, and that should be sufficient."

Somehow things went backward between 1899 and 1957. The good news is, it has improved since 1957. Things have improved even since *Mothers of Invention* was published. Since that time, historian Autumn Stanley released her exhaustively researched *Mothers and Daughters of Invention*. Anne L. Macdonald's *Feminine Ingenuity* traced women innovators' impact on the Industrial Age. Farag Moussa included international inventors in his book *Women Inventors*. Susan Casey's *Women Invent!* and Fred Amram's *From Indian Corn to Outer Space: Women Invent in America* provided a breezy overview of women's practical contributions to science and industry. Ann Fausto-Sterling and Hilary Rose's *Love, Power and Knowledge: Towards a Feminist Transformation of the Sciences* covered the sociological implications of innovative women.

When *Mothers of Invention* came out, there were no women in the National Inventors Hall of Fame. Since that time, we are happy to report, Gertrude Elion, the team of Elizabeth Hazen and Rachel Brown, Stephanie Kwolek, and Helen Murray Free have all seen their work acknowledged and honored there. Women have consistently won the Intellectual Property Owners' National Inventor of the Year Award as well as *Discover* magazine's Discover Award. Statistically, the number of U.S. patents granted in women's names (note: this does not include corporate "work for hire") increased from 1.5 percent in the 1950s, to 2.2 percent in 1977, to 5.6 percent in 1988, to 8 percent in 1993.

Yet when the venerable Smithsonian Institution put out a picture book about inventors for young readers in 1996, it somehow overlooked all the contributions by women that the above-named historians and authors have worked so hard to recognize. *Newsweek* magazine's millennial special, "2000: The Power of Invention," managed to acknowledge exactly two inventions by women: Stephanie Kwolek's Kevlar and Marion Donovan's disposable diaper. It is as if a default setting is being returned to, again and again.

Why is Cyrus McCormick's reaper remembered but not Ann Harned Manning's? Isaac Singer's sewing machine but not Helen Blanchard's? Everyone knows Jonas Salk gave us polio vaccine—how many know that Janet Rideout gave us AZT? Why do people credit Ray Kroc with establishing fast food but never mention that Kate Gleason built the first tract housing? Why do we all know that George Eastman invented the Brownie camera but not that Josephine Cochran invented the dishwasher? That Willis Carrier invented the air conditioner but not that Teri Pall invented the cordless phone?

Names like Colt (guns), Otis (elevators), and Yale (locks) are in the common lexicon, but not Jones (Amanda—vacuum canning), Anderson (Mary—windshield wipers), and Harger (Hannah—the screen door). What would life be like without Mary Phelps "Caresse Crosby" Jacob's bra, Melitta Bentz's drip coffee, or Grace Murray Hopper's user-friendly computer software?

More than a decade after the publication of *Mothers of Invention*, the record still needs to be set straight. Besides, women have been busy inventing new things. Today we can even see the phenomenon of women inventors building on the work of other women inventors. There is a direct line of progress from Hedy Lamarr's frequency-hopping idea to Teri Pall's cordless phone to Randice Altschul's disposable card phone. And look at the relentless battle to cure AIDS: Janet Rideout patented AZT, which was the only treatment until M. Katharine Holloway and Chen Zhao's teams introduced protease inhibitors. Suzanne Ildstad's facilitator-cell technology may one day replace Gertrude Elion's lifesaving immunosuppressant treatment.

Mothers of Invention focused a spotlight on a piece of history that had been locked and forgotten in the attic. Rewardingly, since that time the book has been used in classrooms and women's studies programs across the country. We've also had the privilege of meeting students in our annual lecture series who say the women they read about in *Mothers of Invention* inspired them to pursue studies and careers in science and technology.

In the introduction to our 1988 volume, we speculated that "it is possible to patent your lab-grown AIDS vaccine, as well as the steps required to produce it, and the special hypodermic needed to administer it." At the time that was all the stuff of future fantasy. In this book you will not only meet Janet Rideout, who patented AZT, but Janine Jagger, who patented the virus-proof needles.

We can only guess what predictions made in *Patently Female* will be realized in the next book we write.

—Ethlie Ann Vare and Greg Ptacek

CHAPTER 1

Practicalities

O f necessity, women have long been inventors. The earliest recorded history treated women inventors as deities. The anonymous women gatherers who first cultivated their crops are mythologized by the ancient Greeks as goddess Pallas Athena, "founder of the plow and the plowman's toil." Similarly, China's Se Ling-she, a demigod and wife of Emperor Hwang-te, is credited with discovering silk around 3000 B.C. Queen Semiramis of Assyria is said to have designed the system of canals, causeways, and bridges that made possible the Hanging Gardens of Babylon.

With the advent of the industrial revolution, women began turning their inventive energies toward machinery. Indeed, the first patent granted to a woman in the United States—English Patent #401, awarded to Sybilla Masters in 1715—was for a machine for "cleaning and curing Indian corn." By the early 1800s women were inventing all sorts of practical things. The young nation was still largely rural, so the products of women's imaginations often focused on agriculture. Among the most significant of these were the cotton gin, discussed later in the chapter, and the grain harvester or reaper, which is attributed to Ann Harned Manning in 1843. Later, Cyrus McCormick would become famous when he made further improvements to the machine.

Toward the end of the nineteenth century, women's inventions reflected their new urbanized environments. In 1881 Mary Walton invented a special rail to reduce noise on elevated railways. The Metropolitan Elevated Railway Company of New York City paid her $10,000 plus royalties for her invention. Florence Parpart received Patent #649,609 in 1900 for her "new and useful improvement" in street-cleaning machines. Elizabeth Stiles won first prize in an invention contest sponsored by the Women's Pavilion at the U.S. Centennial celebration in Philadelphia in 1876 for her two-person, multipurpose desk and storage unit—perfect for big-city offices and small apartments.

Despite these practical achievements, the lasting image of women at the turn of this century is the fictional Gibson Girl, who, if she was inclined toward invention at all, would no doubt be bent on making improvements to the fainting couch. That myth isn't supported by the facts. On June 5, 1920, in the wake of women's suffrage, Congress ordered a Women's Bureau to be established in the Department of Labor. One of its first tasks was to do a survey of patents granted to women.

Headed by feminist Mary Anderson (*not* the same Mary Anderson who invented the windshield wiper!), the bureau undertook the formidable study of "how women [have] made material contributions to the sum of achievement." The statistical results were startling: between 1905 and 1920, women were granted hundreds of patents in the areas of manufacturing, structural design, and transportation. Women were found to have invented practicalities ranging from machine-shop tools and power machinery to automobile, railway, and ship parts and accessories; electrical, telephone, and telegraphic equipment; scientific instruments, including meters, scales, and watches; and optical and photographic devices.

Today "necessity" continues to inspire women to invent. Tana Brinnand of Scotts Valley, California, a computer artist who spends most of her day at a keyboard, developed MouseMitts wrist cushions. JoAnn Zucker of Tomkins Cove, New York, was dismayed at the prospect of having to send certified letters to all her neighbors regarding an addition to her home, so she created a "certified phone calling" system. And yes, Virginia, there's even room for one more improvement to the mousetrap: Patent #4,829,704 granted to Josephine Richardson.

Stephanie L. Kwolek
KEVLAR

Thousands of police officers can testify to the value of Stephanie L. Kwolek's breakthrough invention, Kevlar, a synthetic material that's five times as strong as steel. The main ingredient in bulletproof vests, it saved their lives. This polymer fiber is also resistant to wear, corrosion, and flame, which makes it ideal for all protective clothing as well as for ropes and cables used in offshore drilling, in friction products such as brakes, and in aircraft and space-vehicle construction.

Kwolek is credited with the initial discovery of the liquid crystalline polymer solution that led to the high-strength, high-stiffness aramid fiber commercialized by DuPont in 1971. All told, her name appears on sixteen patents, and she is the sole patent holder on seven. She has authored or coauthored twenty-eight scientific publications and won every conceivable award in the field of chemistry, polymers, and plastics engineering.

Chemist Stephanie Kwolek's discovery of a liquid crystalline polymer created a multimillion-dollar industry. (Courtesy of the National Inventors Hall of Fame)

Born July 31, 1923, in New Kensington, Pennsylvania, Kwolek earned her B.A. in chemistry and took a job with E. I. du Pont de Nemours & Company. "I really wanted to study medicine," says Kwolek, "but I didn't have enough money to enter medical school. I joined DuPont as a temporary measure, but the work turned out to be so interesting that I decided to stay on."

Starting as a chemist in the textile-fibers department, Kwolek was promoted through the DuPont ranks. "I think one reason I've stayed so long," she muses, "is that, back in 1946, women were only able to work in the laboratory for a few years; then they pushed us into so-called women's jobs. I had something to prove. Also, I was there at the very beginning when low-temperature polymerization was discovered, and was right there making the discoveries. It was very exciting."

She first gained national recognition in 1960 for her work creating long molecule chains at low temperatures. Her discovery of the technology for spinning fibers from these molecules led to her win of the American Chemical Society Award for Creative Invention, earned her U.S. Patent #3,671,542, and made feasible the commercial production of aramid fibers—a multibillion-dollar industry today. Her patents and many scientific honors are all in the name of "S. L. Kwolek," a reminder of the time when the wrong gender on a byline could be a kiss of death.

The latest honor for the now-retired DuPont scientist came in 1996, when she was named to the National Inventors Hall of Fame. The organization was founded in 1973 to honor individuals who have made major technological advances that contribute to the nation's welfare; past honorees include Thomas Edison, Henry Ford, Louis Pasteur, and Alexander Graham Bell. She continues to serve on the committees of the National Research Council and the National Academy of Sciences

"The path is easier today," Dr. Kwolek tells the young female scientists whom she teaches and encourages. "There are opportunities for women that did not exist when I started working. Then, if a woman spoke her mind, she quickly found herself out of a job."

Catharine Littlefield Greene
Cotton Gin

If Catharine Littlefield Greene had not been instrumental in the creation of the cotton gin, the quintessential American invention, chances are she would have contributed her formidable talents and energy toward some other equally monumental event in U.S. history. That's the kind of woman she was—a colorful figure who lived life on her terms, far beyond the domestic conventions of her early American peers.

Born in 1775 to a leading colonial family, Catharine, or "Caty" as she was known to friends, married Nathaniel Greene, thirteen years her senior and soon to become a trusted aide to General George Washington. Animated and flirtatious, she was an insatiable reader who preferred the company of men, causing tongues to wag throughout colonial society. But she had a serious side as well, following her husband to Valley Forge, where she spent the entire killing winter at his side.

After the war they settled down to antebellum life on Mulberry Grove, the Georgia estate deeded to General Greene by a grateful president. Within a year Nathaniel was dead, and Caty found herself

Though antebellum society frowned upon industrious women, Catharine Littlefield Greene went ahead and led the effort to invent the cotton gin— a machine that revolutionized agriculture. (Courtesy of the Telfair Museum of Art)

in the unenviable position of having to raise five children and manage two plantations alone.

Soon after, the story is told, Caty was at a party at a neighboring plantation when she met Eli Whitney, a Connecticut-born school-teacher in need of a job. She hired him on the spot to tutor her children. She also learned that he was fascinated with mechanical devices, as was she, and challenged him that evening to help her design a machine for "ginning" (deseeding) cotton. As time-consuming as picking cotton was, ginning it was even more so. Whoever could figure out a way of removing human labor from this part of the production process would revolutionize the cotton industry.

Whitney accepted the challenge and in 1792 moved to Mulberry Grove, where he began working on the device between sessions with the children. History is unclear as to exactly how Caty participated in the invention of the cotton gin from this point. Some believe that she actually presented Whitney with a complete set of drawings for the concept. Some insist that her role was confined to suggesting that metal teeth replace the wooden ones built into the gin rollers of his inoperable prototype. Still others say that the invention of the cotton gin was a collaborative effort among Caty, Whitney, and a slave laborer whose name is unrecorded.

What is not disputed is that the gin was her idea and that her money financed the entire engineering process. When the gin was completed, it was Caty Greene who marketed the device to neighboring plantations. That was her first mistake. By the time Whitney had gotten around to patenting the cotton gin in 1794, bootleg copies were already in use throughout the South. Greene exhausted much of her fortune financing Whitney's efforts to protect their proprietary rights in lengthy court battles.

Her second mistake was not insisting that her name be listed on the patent. In spite of her free spirit, putting her name on a patent application was unthinkable to a pre-nineteenth-century woman of her class. Having no proof of her contributions, she stood by and watched Whitney take all the credit. He became famous in his day and, obviously, remembered for centuries. At least her name was listed as one of the cotton gin's licensers, along with the name of her then second husband, Phineas Miller. Unfortunately, the Whitney/Miller cotton gin firm went bankrupt in 1798, having only sold six gins. As Whitney put

Patented in 1794, the cotton gin proved valuable to everyone but its inventor. (Courtesy of the National Museum of American History, Smithsonian Institution)

it, the cotton gin became "an invention . . . so valuable as to be worthless to the inventor."

Miller died five years later, in 1803, leaving Caty again a widow at thirty-nine. In 1807 Whitney was refused an extension on his patent, and patent to the cotton gin became the only one he ever held. Caty died of fever in 1814, her contributions to one of the seminal inventions of the Industrial Age coming to light only late in the twentieth century.

Patricia Billings
GEOBOND

"Sometimes instead of going ahead, you need to go back," says Patricia Billings, seventy-five, who invented a revolutionary new building material called Geobond by researching Renaissance-era manuscripts. The secret to her incredibly strong and heat-resistant, plasterlike substance had been contained in the writings of Michelangelo for centuries. But it took another artist to see the obvious.

Born in Clinton, Missouri, in 1926, Billings studied art at Amarillo College in Texas. In the late 1960s, she opened a shop in Kansas City and began selling her sculptures. Of all the materials she encountered during her art courses, plaster of paris fascinated her the most. Mixed with water, the substance, which is nothing more than heated gypsum, was perfect for making castings. It had one drawback: it wasn't very durable, which she learned the hard way.

After spending four months working on a swan sculpture, she accidentally smashed it. Not in a position where inventory in her shop could simply be swept away, she tried to repair it, first by using more plaster of paris, but the new stuff would not adhere to the old. She even got the bright idea of mixing a little cement into the gypsum, but, as she recalls, "the two materials destroyed each other."

Some years later, on a trip to Italy, she saw for the first time in person the glory of Michelangelo's frescoes, their colors still rich and vibrant after centuries. As an art student she knew that frescoes were simply paint applied to wet plaster. But why the painted frescoes had not faded substantially intrigued her. Studying obscure journals made by the Renaissance masters for their students, she discovered that the plaster used in the frescoes had been strengthened with a cementlike substance—but not cement itself—that changed their chemical components.

After eight years of trial and error in her basement lab, Billings believed she had formulated the correct mixture, which she dubbed Geobond. Ever the artist, she created a ten-inch statue made of Geobond and sent it to a science lab for tests. Eventually the tests would be repeated by no less than the U.S. Air Force, whose scientists discovered that Billings's secret mixture was extremely fire-resistant. To be exact, the material would not burn, even when it was heated to 6,500°F. Even better, it was found that the mixture could be "sculpted" into myriad forms and textures. That made Geobond very attractive to the USAF as a fire-resistant substance for aircraft.

In fact, the unique properties of Geobond make it the first safe alternative to asbestos, the once-standard fire-resistant material whose use was restricted after the 1970s, when it was discovered to cause cancer. Unlike asbestos, Geobond can be hardened and used in place of tile, marble, or bricks. Because it is pourable, it can be used to repair concrete on a bridge or highway . . . or even fix a broken swan statue.

The milky-looking substance is being manufactured through a small company Billings established in her hometown of Kansas City with start-up capital borrowed from friends. Recently the diminutive, bespectacled great-grandmother turned down a $20 million buyout offer from a company she was convinced would bury the technology. While Geobond International is just breaking even, Billings estimates that her five-year-old company will soon be generating upwards of $260 million in net profits.

Bette Nesmith Graham
LIQUID PAPER

There are some things a desk just can't do without. A stapler, for instance (invented by Charles Henry Gould in 1868), a paper clip (Johaan Valer, 1900), or a bottle of Liquid Paper (Bette Nesmith

The ubiquitous office product Liquid Paper began as a cottage industry in the garage of Bette Nesmith Graham, a secretary and single mom. She's pictured here with son Michael Nesmith, who later became famous as one of the members of sixties' pop group The Monkees. (Courtesy of Michael Nesmith)

Graham, 1951). That Bette Nesmith was a single mom in postwar Texas, working as a secretary when she created the correction fluid that would eventually earn her $47.5 million (in 1976 dollars) is one of the great stories of American enterprise. That her son would become a rock-and-roll superstar just adds to the lore.

Turn back the clock for a moment. It's 1951, and Bette is in her office at the Texas Bank & Trust in Dallas. She has risen through the ranks to become an executive secretary, which back then was about as high as the glass ceiling went for women in the banking industry. Indeed, that she there at all was an anomaly.

Like so many young women of her generation, she had married her high school sweetheart just as he was about to go off to war. But unlike the lives of her peers, who after the war were busy at home raising the kids who would later become the Baby Boom generation, Bette's life took an odd turn. She and her husband, Warren, divorced in 1946. With no other way to support little Michael, she had to go to work.

It's perhaps difficult to realize that not too many years ago a divorced woman in the United States was instantly stigmatized. "Grass widows," they called them. A single mother in religiously conservative Texas might as well have branded a big D on her blouse. And then to top everything off, *it* arrived, and any sense of financial security Bette had suddenly slipped away.

"It" was the newfangled electric typewriter from IBM. With their carbon-film ribbons and lightning-quick touch, these typewriters mass-produced typographical errors—and left behind a terrible mess when you tried to erase one. And despite her title, Bette did not actually excel at secretarial skills. It was only a matter of time.

The answer to her problem came through her love of painting. A talented art student in high school, she longed to pursue her ambition someday. In the meantime she earned extra money by helping to design the holiday windows at the bank. And that's when the lightbulb clicked on.

"With lettering, an artist never corrects by erasing, but always paints over the error," recalled Nesmith. "So I decided to use what artists use. I put some tempera water-base paint in a bottle and took my watercolor brush to the office. And I used that to correct my mistakes."

For almost five years Bette would sneak her bottle of white paint out of the drawer and correct her typos. It was considered cheating, a way of passing herself off as a better typist than she was. Once, when she changed jobs, her new boss admonished her, "Don't use any of that white stuff on my letters." The boss might not have approved, but the gals in the typing pool knew a good thing when they saw it. After the umpteenth co-worker asked Bette for a bottle of her magic potion, she went home and made the first batch of what the hand-painted label called "Mistake Out." Son Michael would help her fill the bottles out in the garage, and she consulted his chemistry teacher for advice on making the formula cover better and dry faster.

Over the next decade Liquid Paper would establish itself as an essential part of any office (and Michael would establish himself as a teen sensation in the Monkees). By 1979, when the Gillette Corporation offered to buy Bette's company for a price she could not refuse, the Liquid Paper company employed two hundred people, producing 25 million bottles a year that were distributed to thirty-one countries. Bette devoted the rest of her life to her two passions: Christian Science and art.

When she died in 1980, she was worth almost $50 million. Half her inheritance went to her son, and the other half to her foundations, one of which was the first devoted exclusively to promoting women in the arts.

Patricia A. Bianconi
Artificial Diamonds

The idea of whipping up a tiara in the lab before a big night on the town never crossed her mind when Patricia A. Bianconi created the first artificial diamond. She swears.

Bianconi, an assistant professor of chemistry at Pennsylvania State University, says the idea first came from trying to make polymers for the manufacture of computer chips. With her graduate-student assistant, Glenn Visher, she began experimenting by adding carbon to their favorite polymer recipe. "We were just really [trying] to see if we could make these chemical curiosities, and suddenly the thought struck: 'All these carbons are tetrahedral, just like in diamonds. Do you think if we heated it, you know, it would turn into a diamond?'"

Curiosity got the better of them, and they decided to try it just once. After a quick bake in the oven at 450°C, the polymer was indeed transformed into a diamond.

Admittedly Bianconi's oven-baked diamonds are not gemstone quality. The shiny black material looks more like graphite than the gift that lasts forever. But in terms of its molecular structure it's almost identical to any other diamond, which makes it extremely valuable for industrial use.

Diamonds, of course, are the hardest known material, natural or man-made, which makes them ideal for drills or for anything you might want to make scratchproof. But their scarcity, and ergo their high cost, makes them impractical for wide-scale industrial use. Plus, natural diamonds are not malleable.

Imagine, however, being able to coat windshields with scratch-proof diamond surfaces. While Bianconi says "it will take a lot of development before it's a really viable commercial thing," this modern-day alchemist plans on continuing to tinker with the original formula. Tiffany & Co., watch out.

Martine Kempf
VOICE-CONTROLLED DEVICES

Even before the advent of the first practical computer in the 1950s, scientists and writers had dreamed of machines that would respond to "their master's voice." The vision became popularized in film and television: think of Hal in *2001: A Space Odyssey* (whose responses were admittedly idiosyncratic) and the friendly robot in television's *Lost in Space*.

In reality, however, there was a vexing problem associated with voice-recognition computer commands: everyone's voice is different, which means that a computer would have to anticipate what every human being's voice might sound like. And that's a logistical nightmare, if not a mathematical impossibility.

Martine Kempf, the inventor of the first voice-controlled devices,

Martine Kempf, inventor of the first voice-controlled devices, was only twenty-seven when she patented the microprocessor called the Katalavox. (Courtesy of Michele Mattei)

likened the problem of different voices to leaves on a tree. "They might seem the same, but two leaves are never exactly alike. The human brain can quickly figure out that while two leaves are not exactly alike, they are similar enough not to give them a second thought. Computers, however, do not possess that relational ability."

So how did she overcome the problem to create voice-activated devices ranging from surgical microscopes to wheelchairs? Her solution was elegantly simple: the user programs his or her voice into the microprocessors that control the devices. Thus the computer has to "memorize" only a singular voice.

Kempf was a twenty-three-year-old astronomy student in 1982 when she first designed a computer program that would respond to spoken commands. By the time she was twenty-seven, her patented microprocessing invention, the Katalavox (from the Greek *katal*, "to understand," and the Latin *vox*, meaning "voice") was being manufactured in her own factory in California's Silicon Valley. The Katalavox proved to be twenty times more efficient than comparable models that established computer firms had been perfecting for years.

Raised in the Alsace-Lorraine region of France, Kempf attended university at Bonn, Germany. Her invention was inspired by her father, a polio victim who designed a hand-controlled automobile for his own use and later made a business of customizing cars for the handicapped. She began to work on the voice activator when she saw armless German teenagers, thalidomide victims, who had no way to maneuver their wheelchairs. A wheelchair that responded to voice commands seemed the solution. (Thalidomide was a drug that was marketed in the 1950s as a sleeping pill and to treat morning sickness during pregnancy. Tragically, it was later discovered to cause severe birth defects and resulted in the birth of thousands of deformed babies, many with no or stunted limbs.)

Over the years Kempf has continued to refine her voice-controlled devices. Recently she improved upon her father's work to make an electronic hand-controlled accelerator and automatic clutch for disabled drivers. She received the Prix Grand Siècle Laurent Perrier for her contribution to microsurgery. Still, she makes time to pursue varied interests, which include piloting her own plane and playing classical piano, violin, and bassoon.

As a woman engineer, she makes a point of visiting grade-school classrooms to "tell both boys and girls that it is definitely cool to be smart." She avoids the term "feminist" but uses the school forum as an opportunity to drive home the idea that women as well as men can be entrepreneurs, scientists, engineers, and inventors. "I don't believe men and women think that differently. By and large the reason women are underrepresented in the fields of science and technology is cultural. Even today I am amazed by friends who begin the acculturation process by virtually forbidding their girls from playing with anything remotely mechanical."

Among the most rewarding aspects of her technology is the direct impact it has upon its recipients. She receives letters and photographs from disabled boys and girls about how grateful they are to have the freedom of mobility because of their voice-activated wheelchairs. However, her favorite story is of an elderly quadriplegic man who used his voice-activated wheelchair to travel throughout the world. "He had been dreaming of such a device for twenty years," she said.

Mary Anderson
WINDSHIELD WIPER

It was the turn of the last century in New York City, and Mary Anderson of Birmingham, Alabama, was sightseeing—riding in an electric-powered streetcar. The thoroughly modern device was truly a man-made miracle, allowing cheap, fast, and easy transportation between destinations.

For a lady like Miss Anderson, whose ankle-length skirts and corset were still largely the product of nineteenth-century fashion, the prospect of not having to climb onto a horse-drawn buggy to ride across town must have seemed a godsend. As she sat in her comfortable seat, Anderson might have reflected upon the remarkable march of progress that she was witnessing—the lightbulb, the phonograph, the telephone, the radio, and mechanical refrigeration—all were invented between 1850 and 1903.

What next, machines that will fly? she might have thought. However, sitting up front in the streetcar, she could not help but notice a slight flaw in the design of the marvelous rapid-transit vehicle. The gathering snow was piling up on the windshield, making it impossible for the conductor to see. The poor man would have to lean out and brush the snow away with his bare hands, obviously uncomfortable and possibly dangerous for the passengers. No, there had to be a better way.

On June 18, 1903, Mary Anderson joined the turn of the century's amazing march of progress when she filed a patent with the U.S. Patent Office for a "window-cleaning device" or, as she described it, "a simple mechanism for removing snow, rain and sleet from the glass in front of a motorman."

Her invention consisted of a wiper mounted on the outside of the windshield that could be moved manually by a handle mounted inside. According to her patent application, the wiper utilized a "rubber T, adapted to sweep across and clean the window-pane . . . with yielding and uniform pressure upon the glass." This was achieved by an elegant piece of engineering that utilized a counterweight, a spindle, and interlocks. One suspects that Miss Anderson was a bit of a perfectionist, because she designed her device to be "easily removable when not required, thus leaving nothing to mar the usual appearance of the car during fair weather." In any case, it's evident she was quite proud of her apparatus, summarizing in her application that "the difficulty of not being able to see through the front glass in stormy weather is effectually obviated."

A few months after she filed her application, she received Patent #743,801. It's impossible to calculate what licensing fees for such a basic device might be worth in today's dollars. Unfortunately, history does not record whether Mary Anderson profited handsomely, or at all, from her sole foray into the world of invention. But we do know that she lived well, because when she died in 1953 at the age of eighty-seven, it was at her "summer home" in Tennessee.

Amanda Theodosia Jones / Mary Engle Pennington
Vacuum Canning

After several largely unsuccessful careers as a feminist educator, psychic spiritualist, and poet, Amanda Theodosia Jones hit pay dirt with a prosaic glass jar. In 1872 Miss Jones conceived of a vacuum process for preserving food. Her "Jones exhauster" (the name would never catch on) was awarded Patents #139,547, #139,580, and #140,247 for a system in which food was placed in a container, the air drained out through a series of valves, and hot (100 to 120°F) liquid added to the container to complete the seal.

Jones's vacuum-canning process revolutionized food preservation, a cause of great concern to a nation that was rapidly changing from rural to urban. Her invention allowed, for the first time, fresh food to be stored in quantity without having to cook all the flavor out of it. Everything from lunch meat to tapioca pudding was soon being manufactured with Jones's process—much of it at her female-owned and operated U.S. Women's Pure Food Vacuum Preserving Company in Chicago.

Mary Engle Pennington was born the year that Jones filed her first vacuum-canning patents. Twenty-five years later Pennington would again revolutionize the food industry with her patents for refrigeration.

Unlike her predecessor, Pennington was quite sure she wanted to be a scientist from a very early age—during an era that looked upon women scientists as at best an oddity and at worst an abomination against God. Completing her bachelor of science requirements at the University of Pennsylvania, Pennington was refused a degree because of her gender. Undaunted, she continued her postgraduate studies with such stellar performance that she eventually shamed the faculty into awarding her a Ph.D. She may be the only person refused a bachelor's degree but awarded a doctorate from the same university.

Unable to find employment (that gender problem again), she opened her own business, the Philadelphia Clinical Laboratory, specializing in bacteriology. Her research into food spoilage brought her to the attention of the chief chemist of the U.S. Department of Agriculture, and he knew that her talents would be invaluable at the government level. He also knew that the department would never hire a woman.

So "M. E. Pennington" took and passed the civil service exam, and soon "Mr. Pennington" was welcomed into the U.S. Food Research Laboratory, where he . . . ah, she specialized in studying the spoilage of foods. Even today spoilage is a matter of grave concern; think of the recent deaths due to *E. coli* contamination. At the beginning of the twentieth century, when Pennington set up shop, bacteria felled thousands of people annually, especially during the summer in large cities.

Cold temperature kills most bacteria. But the problem with early refrigeration systems was that as the temperature dropped inside the food locker, humidity was lost and the food dried out. Increase humidity and the food spoiled. There was no point making the food bacteria-free if no one was inclined to eat it.

Pennington solved the problem of humidity control. Her innovations in refrigeration were so vital that during World War I she was awarded a Notable Service Medal by President Herbert Hoover.

Teri Pall
CORDLESS PHONE

The holder of thirty-three patents for devices as varied as a solar cooker, a wrist chronograph calculator, and a miniature electronic pain blocker, Teri Pall is best known for an item that has become part of virtually every modern household. "I invented the first cordless phone in 1965, but I couldn't market it," Pall recently explained to *Inventors' Digest* magazine. Why not? She laughed. "It had a two-mile radius and would interfere with aircraft."

In 1968 she sold the rights to a manufacturer that "dumbed down" the technology to limit its range. Today Pall is recognized as having single-handedly begun the cordless-communication revolution that allowed us to walk and talk at the same time.

Yet the world almost got Teri Pall the bass player rather than Teri Pall the inventor. Not only did she finance her college education playing in a progressive-jazz trio, but after college the Teri Pall Trio was even represented by the William Morris talent agency. Engagements were booked throughout the United States and Europe, and Pall considered making music her career.

But no. Teri Pall was born to invent. When she was a child, her father always encouraged her to be curious, "to take things apart and see what makes them tick." Her first invention involved the family radio. "It was receiving two stations simultaneously," she recalled. "I took it apart and created a modified tuning device, which eliminated the problem."

At the time her family was living in Princeton, New Jersey, and the company that manufactured the radio was headquartered in New York City. Even though she was only twelve years old, "I decided that they should know about my improvement," said Pall. "So I made an appointment to see one of the executives. I carried my modification to New York in a cigar box. After I demonstrated it to him, he said, 'What do you want us to do with it?' I responded that I thought they should buy it. 'Well,' he said, 'I'll give you one thousand dollars.' "

Flabbergasted that her simple little modification might result in such a windfall, Pall repeated back the sum to the executive. "'A thousand dollars?' He thought I was insulted and said, 'I'll make it two thousand dollars—but that's my final offer.' I quickly accepted!"

So, despite the jazz combo, despite doctorates in both paleontology and physics from Columbia University and London's Imperial College, Teri Pall invents.

"First and foremost I consider myself a scientist, and scientific methods are exactly what are needed to be an inventor. When I go out on a 'dig,' which may last two or three months, my job is to dig for facts and start to put things together. That's what inventors do, too," she said.

Pall has a simple theory about inventing: make it and then move on. Too many inventors become obsessed with and paranoid about the products of their imagination, she said. She also thinks having a thick skin helps. "The biggest challenge for inventors is overcoming despondency when their invention is rejected. What they have to do is analyze the rejection and ask themselves what they can do to improve [the invention]."

Determined to share with others the lessons that she learned, Pall cofounded the Inventors Guild of America, a nonprofit organization based in Van Nuys, California. The guild helped its members with the nuts and bolts of getting their ideas to market. While the organization is now defunct, a victim of the Northridge earthquake, she urges readers of this book to join one of the many other nonprofits that exist to assist inventors. (See Appendix B.)

In a world of rapidly changing technology that some find intimidating, Pall sees nothing but bright horizons, especially for those with inventive minds. "There's so much we can do," she said, "and so much that needs to be done."

Martha Coston
MARITIME SIGNAL FLARE

The signal flare that we traditionally call a "Very pistol"—a safety device no ship would be without—was not invented by Lt. E. W. Very, after whom it is named. Lieutenant Very patented a small adjustment to the trigger mechanism. The signal flare itself was patented by Martha Coston, a young widow who perfected the device mostly in an effort to support her three children.

And even though there are some who credit Coston's advance in ship-to-ship communications with helping the Union win the Civil War, the Department of the Navy not only denied her the honor of naming it after her but even shortchanged her on the payment.

"We hear much of the chivalry of men towards women," Coston wrote in her 1886 autobiography, "but let me tell you, gentle reader, it vanishes like dew before the summer sun when one of us comes into competition with the manly sex. . . . It was a most bitter thing to find

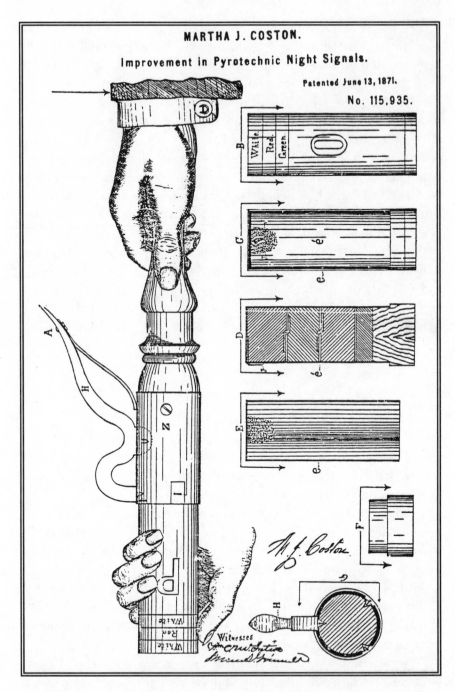

It took Martha Coston ten years to perfect the signal flare that was eventually adopted by navies around the world.

in that lofty institution of our country, the Navy, men so small-minded that they begrudged a woman her success."

Born in Baltimore and raised in Philadelphia, Martha Hunt eloped with the brilliant young engineer Benjamin Coston when she was only fourteen. She was just twenty-one when he died of pneumonia, leaving her with a bankrupt business and three small children. Her best hope was the trunkful of pyrotechnics Benjamin had been working with when he died—including an early, nonworking prototype of the signal flare.

It took ten years of work for Martha to perfect the device, work made that much harder by her gender. She used a man's name when she wrote to fireworks manufacturers to get the necessary chemical flares. The navy wouldn't allow her to attend the tests of her own device. Eventually the navy ordered $6,000 worth of Coston Telegraphic Night Signals and later gave her $20,000 for the rights. She had to sue them for the money. She subsequently patented the device in England, France, Holland, Austria, Denmark, Italy, and Sweden, often traveling around Europe with her explosive wares in a trunk labeled "music boxes." She often joked that in the whole world, only Denmark treated her fairly.

Coston's surviving sons continued what became a successful manufacturing business, but Martha went to her grave regretting that her family never got the credit they deserved for their contribution to the sailors of the world.

Kate Gleason

TRACT HOUSING

Born at the close of the Civil War, Kate Gleason would leave an indelible mark on the landscape of the twentieth century. For better or for worse, she invented mass-produced, low-cost tract housing.

Her real estate development in Rochester, New York, in 1921 offered the public 101 houses, each composed of six rooms, complete with gas range, built-in bookcases, and ironing boards, for the mere cost of $40 a month. And, as with Henry Ford's Model T, buyers could have any style they wanted as long as it was the one style being offered.

The parallel between Gleason's housing development and the automobile industry was more than coincidental. She actually was inspired to mass-produce homes "from a visit I made to the Cadillac factory, when Mr. Leland showed me the assembly of the eight cylinder engine," she once wrote.

Gleason would go on to build several other housing developments before dying in 1933 at age sixty-eight, a wealthy and respected general contractor.

Margaret Knight/Lydia Deubener
THE PAPER BAG

Although she patented a total of twenty-seven separate inventions in her lifetime, Margaret Knight is best known for a machine that makes flat-bottomed paper bags. Knight's 1870 patent was a highly

The original model of Margaret Knight's paper-bag making machine is on display at the Smithsonian Institution. (Photo by Sandra A. Brick from the Abram/Brick Woman Inventor Collection)

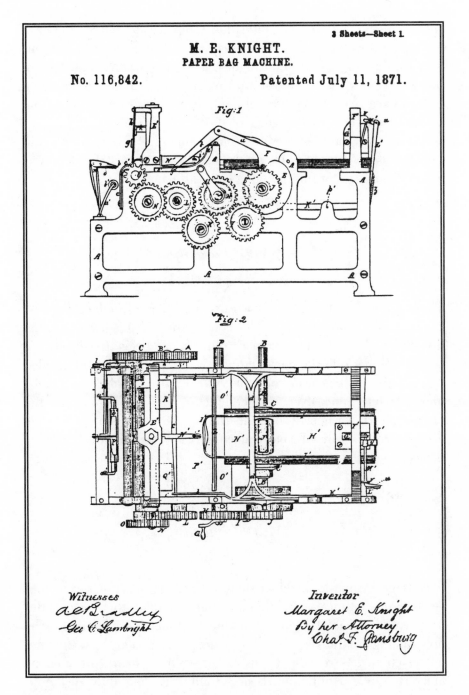

Margaret Knight was forced to defend her patent in court: contemporary manufacturers couldn't believe a woman actually invented a useful machine.

successful one that has been refined over the decades but is still in use today. Her original model is on display at the Smithsonian Institution.

A kind of "Lady Edison," Knight would go on to invent all sorts of mechanical devices before the turn of the twentieth century, ranging from valves and rotors for automobile engines to leather-cutting devices used in the manufacture of shoes.

Almost fifty years later a Minnesotan named Lydia Deubener would improve upon Knight's invention. In 1918 she filed for and was awarded a patent for the shopping bag with handles.

Emily Goss Davenport
ELECTRIC MOTOR

Thomas and Emily Davenport worked together to produce the first small electric motor in 1834. Her contribution to this invention that literally sped up the industrial revolution has been trivialized to a story about her offering her wedding gown to provide the silk needed to wind the motor's iron core. In truth, Emily provided the crucial idea of using quicksilver as a conductor. This finally enabled the motor to turn a wheel. Today the Davenport motor continues to be used to drive all sorts of factory machinery and household laborsaving devices, as well as the electric car.

Mary Howell
THE AIRCART

Ever since Leonardo da Vinci sketched a flying machine, each succeeding generation has attempted to improve upon the concept. But despite early-twentieth-century prognostications that had all of us by now zipping around via jet pack or helicopter, a practical personal flying machine has remained elusive. Enter the Aircart, invented by Mary Howell of Huntington Beach, California. This nifty all-terrain vehicle (Patent #4,666,012)—a combination motorcycle, snowmobile, and jet ski—transports the user on a cushion of compressed air.

A mother of three who also holds a patent for a rail-mounted camera system, Howell looks to the day when every household will have an Aircart in their garage. "It would be great," she says. "Think of the money we could save on road repair!"

Carmemina Parkhurst
AUTOMATED MOTEL

It's a good guess that Carmemina Parkhurst's invention will never be embraced by hotel employee unions. But for the weary traveler, it might be a godsend. The resident of Fortuna, California, received Patent #5,463,546 for an "automatic motel clerk," a device that works along the lines of self-ticketing machines found at train stations and airports. Guests would choose a room based on photographs, then press a button under the appropriate picture. After entering a valid credit card number, "a key would come out with a receipt and all the information about check-in and check-out times," she says.

Granted, this approach may not satisfy those looking for a night at the Ritz, but conceivably many innkeepers will be attracted to the prospect of "not having to pay out salaries, overtime, vacation benefits, and other types of expenses" that come with human workers.

Doris Drucker
VOICE MONITOR

Doris Drucker will never be accused of being sedentary. When she was sixty-nine, she went on a trek through Nepal. When she was eighty, the Los Angeles–area resident patented the Visivox, a battery-powered monitoring device that visually cues a speaker when his or her voice drops below an audible level. Doris got the idea when her husband, a public speaker, developed a hearing problem and could no longer tell when his voice was trailing off. At first she would sit in the audience and wave when she could no longer hear him. Frustrated with that arrangement, she looked for a device to do the job. When she realized there was no such thing, she patented one. A Visivox weighs about ten pounds and sells for just under $500; to date more than one hundred have been purchased by professional speakers and speech therapists.

Harriet Hosmer
CULTURED MARBLE

A world-famous sculptor in her day, Harriet Hosmer received five patents for mechanical devices, as well as the first patent for artificial marble. Born in Watertown, Massachusetts, Hosmer was reared to be an independent thinker by her father, a physician who became a widower when she was four. As a student, young Harriet excelled in the art of sculpture and by twenty-six was receiving commissions from public institutions for her neoclassical sculptures. Besides her cultured marble, praised by building contractors at the time, she created a page-turning device for musicians and ultimately became obsessed with creating the impossible: a perpetual motion machine.

"Anyone can do sculpture," said the overly modest Hosmer after a celebrated career as an artist. "What I try for now is original work."

Sandy Flick
CAR TRAY TABLE

Traffic safety experts say you shouldn't eat in a moving car. They've obviously never driven with a typical American family, says Sandy Flick. A "frustrated mother, fed up with the mess in the car and on the children's clothes whenever eating en route," Flick invented the Lap Top Commuter, a kind of TV tray for the car.

A year after a sharp turn caused a fast-food hamburger and fries to end up on her good skirt, she developed a prototype for her invention. Then she hit the road on a unique ten-thousand-mile marketing campaign, in which she invited the regional purchasing officers of every major fast food chain to dine with her "à la car," proving that their customers needed her device. The Lap Top Commuter is now available nationwide through select retailers.

Celeste Baranski

PERSONAL COMMUNICATOR

The 1990s ushered in the era of personal communication. Pagers, cell phones, and notebook computers allowed for truly mobile offices, so that workers—or loved ones—could keep in touch wherever they might be. Yet with all the technological wizardry, something as simple as sending a map with directions to a client was impossible to do outside the office. Or fax documents. Or e-mail messages. What we needed was a desktop that you could carry in a suitcase. . . .

Celeste Baranski made it happen with her invention of the personal communicator. In 1993, together with colleague Alain Rossman, she devised an integrated cellular phone, fax machine, and pen-input personal computer—a quantum leap for mobile communication. It was the first of the personal digital assistants that today have became de rigueur for any savvy business traveler.

"There was no model to go by; there was no accumulated wisdom from previous products, " she recalled in a recent interview. Named appropriately the Personal Communicator, the device offered a day planner, a phone book with autodialer, and a note-taking program that could also handle basic handwriting recognition for transforming notes into e-mail.

As vice president of hardware engineering for EO, a Mountain View, California firm that was funded by AT&T and Matsushita, Baranski was involved with the project from the start. Miniaturizing so much equipment to fit into the palm of a hand was not the only challenge. Since both phone and computers emit radio signals, a means for eliminating interference had to be developed. Then the marketing department declared that the entire system had to power up in less than five seconds. "It could not behave like a typical computer. Nobody would wait for two or three minutes for this type of system to boot," she said.

The end result was that the Personal Communicator performed

better than most desktop computers. Baranski and Rossman won the coveted 1993 Discover Award from *Discover* magazine for their invention.

Randice Altschul
DISPOSABLE PHONE

Where are inventions likely to be conceived? When the proverbial lightbulb switches on, are inventors apt to be in the laboratory? Or perhaps in bed, after a refreshing night's sleep? How about just sitting and reading?

For Randice Altschul, age forty, it was none of the above. She conceived of the disposable phone while driving along a highway one day in 1996. Having entered one of the so-called roaming zones that plague wireless telephony, she was ready to chuck her worthless cell phone out the car window—until she realized how much the darn thing cost. That's when it hit her. Why not create a phone so cheap that one wouldn't be reluctant to just throw it away?

Crazy, huh? Like a fox. As we go to press, her Phone-Card-Phone is about to go into production at three factories with orders for 100 million of the devices. Her goal: nothing less than to be the next Bill Gates.

If you think her disposable phone is just a novelty—the digital equivalent of the Pet Rock—think again. The technological advances embodied by the twenty-two patents that she filed on behalf of the Phone-Card-Phone represent "a profound change in the design of electronic" gadgetry, so "startlingly functional" that it will "very probably spell the death of pay phones," according to the *Los Angeles Times*.

The disposable phone as conceived by Altschul, when folded, is the size of a credit card. Unrolling it reveals a fully functional keypad, microphone, and receiver. The product is based on her Super Thin Technology, which allows a standard electronic circuit to be printed on any material using magnetic ink. There's no need to make the phone rugged because there are no moving parts or wires to protect.

The Phone-Card-Phone is packed with sixty minutes of calling time and even comes with a hands-free attachment. When the sixty minutes are used, you can add more minutes or throw the device away.

Who's the brain behind this technological breakthrough? In one sense, she is the most unlikely of candidates. Her background is in toy and game design. At age twenty-five, she persuaded the executive producer of the *Miami Vice* television series to let her create a Miami Vice Game. She then invented Barbie's 30th Birthday Game and a wearable stuffed toy. Her next invention, which still has to be marketed, was really out-of-the-box: the world's first "edible toy figure constructed of breakfast cereal."

"The greatest asset I have over everyone else in business is my toy mentality," she recently told the *New York Times*. "An engineer's mentality is to make something last, to make it durable. A toy's life span is about an hour, then the kid throws it away. You get it, you play with it and—boom—it's gone."

After her highway epiphany she hired a team of engineers and in November 1999 was issued her first patent on the disposable phone. A year later she had the first working model of the Phone-Card-Phone developed. A savvy businesswoman as well as a creative mind, she is the president and founder of Dieceland Technologies, the manufacturer of the Phone-Card-Phone, and she personally raised the funding needed to take the product to market.

She says that she comes up with as many as twenty to thirty new ideas a week. Her motto: "Conceive It! Believe It! Achieve It!" For the time being, however, she is focusing on other products utilizing her Super Thin Technology. Up next? A disposable laptop computer that will retail for $20. Are you listening, Mr. Gates?

And Let's Not Forget . . .

Asa Devlin Foster of Minneapolis, Minnesota, received Patent #4,853,675 for "an apparatus for determining impact force upon a vehicle traveling in a curve." The device mounts on the vehicle and, essentially, warns you if you're about to tip over—a godsend to first-time drivers of the ever-increasing numbers of sports utility vehicles. . . . During the 1800s, trains and trolleys frequently ran off their tracks when the bolts holding the rails together came undone through normal wear and tear. **Catherine Ryan** patented an idea in 1904, which became an industry standard, for a locking nut that would permanently hold the bolt in place. She got the idea when she noticed how her wedding ring was caught behind the joint of her finger. . . . **Anna W. Keichline,** the first registered female architect in New York State, patented a number of practical items, including a compressed-air radiator and dryer. In the 1980s her great-niece **Nancy Perkins** followed in Keichline's footsteps, receiving patents for an improved car battery and other hardware. . . . In 1879 **Anna Baldwin** patented "the cow milker," a hand-operated suction machine that was either the world's first milking machine or close to it (historical opinions disagree). Baldwin also patented an alcoholic beverage made with brown sugar that had its fans (historical drinkers also disagreed). . . . Lyme disease, which is transmitted by deer ticks, is a serious health hazard in forty-three states. **Susan Luria,** with her husband, Neil, invented the Tick and Small Crawling Creature Barrier, an adjustable adhesive bracelet that captures the creepy critters. . . . In the late 1800s the U.S. House of Representatives adopted an electric gong-and-switch system for signaling pages. Developed by **Miriam Benjamin,** the system for the first time allowed debates to continue without interruption. . . . **Susan Huhn** of Groton, Massachusetts, invented an electronic, chad-proof voting machine that is easier to operate and more accurate than its predecessors. First used in 1977 in Boston, Huhn's machine weighs only thirty-five pounds, is collapsible for transport, and can instantly detect voting errors. . . . While riding as a child in the 1880s, **Annie Chilton** discovered the hard way that a gunshot can cause a horse to bolt and pull the carriage along with it. In 1891, the grown-up Annie received a patent for the Horse Detacher and Brake. . . . **Therese Luce** and **Miriam Bottinick** both had the same goal: make riding in a car safer for pets. They came up with different solutions. Luce's Animal Safety Belt is a five-way adjustable seat belt that works with a car's existing passenger-restraint system. Bottinick's Pet Restrainer for Car Safety is a device placed between the front bucket seats of a car that confines Fido to the backseat. . . . **Jean Bergh** was coinventor of the Goodyear Aquatred tire, which won a Distinguished Inventors Award from the Intellectual Property Owners in 1993. . . . Analytical chemist **Michelle Buchanan** used her background in mass spectrometry to create the first kid-sensitive fingerprint kit. (Children's fingerprints contain more volatile chemicals, which make them disappear faster—a major problem for law enforcement.) Buchanan's technology is now used for everything from detecting chemical weapons to screening for genetic disease. . . . **Janet Mitchell,** head of research projects for Airbus, has invented along with her team an entirely new type of welding. The patented "Friction Stir" process uses intense friction rather than heat to bond metals together. Materials are softened just to the point before they liquefy, allowing molecules to be stirred together before hardening again. The technique is being used on the A3XX, Airbus' new double-decker, super-jumbo airliner.

CHAPTER 2

"Woman's Work"

W e put "woman's work" in quotes because the concept is, today, pretty laughable. In the new millennium, women's work ranges from astrophysics to zoology. Women are carpenters and cantors, sailors and steelworkers, pilots and professors. But there's good historical reason that the textile-making art gave us terms like "distaff" and "spinster": women have always had primary responsibility for home and hearth.

An anthropological survey of 185 different societies, primitive and advanced, found food preparation to be an exclusively female endeavor in 117 and primarily female in 63. (If you're adding along, you've noticed that somewhere on this planet there are 5 societies where food is primarily or exclusively prepared by men. We'll let you know when we locate them.)

None of this frantic housekeeping stops women from inventing, however. Take Harriet Irwin: she invented the whole house. Indeed, when Irwin patented her then-futuristic hexagonal house in 1869, 440 of the 94,116 patents granted to date were in women's names.

At that time, the bulk of patents granted to women were for wearing apparel, culinary utensils, and "sewing and spinning." More than half the patents could be considered household items. Times change. In a 1923 survey conducted by the Women's Bureau of the Department of Labor, only 27 percent of the by then more than five thousand patents granted to women could be considered household goods.

Note the difference in a survey by the U.S. Patent and Trademark Office covering the years 1977–1988. By far the largest number of patents granted to women was in the field of biochemistry. Food and apparel commanded percentages close to those of "information storage and retrieval" and "radiation imagery." And as many patents were granted to women in this eleven-year period as in the first eighty years of the Patent Office's existence.

But though we embrace the change, let's not denigrate the importance of women's contributions to cooking, cleaning, and sewing. It's good that Ellen Demorest and Eleanor Butterick invented paper dress patterns. (Guess which one thought to patent the idea!) It's good that Ruth Wakefield accidentally invented the chocolate chip cookie and ushered in the chocolate chip itself. (Today more than a quarter of all cookies eaten contain chocolate chips.) It's good that Mary Potts patented the cold-handled sadiron ("sad" meant "heavy," and Potts's invention was the first iron consumers could actually pick up without burning themselves.)

So thank you, Amanda Theodosia Jones for inventing vacuum canning, and Dorothy Rodgers for inventing the Jonny Mop. Thank you, Mary Pennington, for perfecting refrigeration and thank you, Hannah Harger, for inventing the screen door.

It wouldn't feel like home without you.

Josephine Cochran
AUTOMATIC DISHWASHER

No one could be surprised that a woman invented the first practical automatic dishwasher. Who else needed one? But it's interesting that the inventor of such an everyday item hasn't been recorded in the history books the way, for instance, the inventor of the sewing machine has been. Perhaps if a *Joseph* Cochran had sold the first dishwashing machine, instead of a *Josephine*, the books would read differently.

Josephine Garis Cochran (she sometimes affected the spelling "Cochrane") was not the first person to come up with the idea of a dishwashing device, nor even the first to patent one. The first dishwasher patent on record was issued to another woman: Mary Hobson, back in 1870—and even then it contained the word "improved." In fact, a dozen dishwasher patents, all of them held by women, predate Josephine Cochran's 1886 model. But it was Cochran—from Illinois by way of Ohio, the daughter of an engineer and wife of a circuit clerk—who designed the first automatic dishwashing machine that worked well enough to be mass-produced and sold.

Josephine and William Cochran lived a comfortable life in Shelbyville, Illinois—comfortable enough that Josephine's biggest problem was the maid's breaking her heirloom china. All that changed in 1883, when William died suddenly, leaving Josephine with $1,535 in assets, $2,769 in debts—and a great idea for a dishwashing machine. The idea was simple: water pressure. Aim soapy water at the dishes and let the suds do the work. Josephine retired to the woodshed (there's a historical marker on the spot) and started assembling copper tubing.

Resembling a big glass box with racks for plates and glasses, the Garis-Cochran Dishwasher came in a small foot-pedal model and a large steam-driven version. The big machine was capable of washing and drying two hundred dishes in two minutes. It was miraculous, the sensation of the 1892 Columbian Exhibition. It was also expensive. At $250 a pop, the dishwasher was too costly for all but commercial use. As Cochran noted sadly in an interview shortly before her death in 1913, the person actually washing the dishes "isn't the deciding factor when it comes to spending comparatively large sums of money for the house."

Still, the Garis-Cochran Washing Machine Company sold enough of them to hotels and restaurants to keep itself in business throughout Josephine Cochran's lifetime. The company was sold in 1926 and its name changed to KitchenAid—now a division of the Whirpool Corporation.

Melitta Bentz

DRIP COFFEEMAKER

At the beginning of the twentieth century making coffee was a messy job. Coffee grounds were wrapped in a cloth bag and then steeped in boiling water. It was a time-consuming process, and half the time the grounds leaked out of the bag, turning the coffee grainy and bitter. If you were in a hurry, you could always simply throw loose grounds in water and boil it . . . and isn't your nose already wrinkling at the thought of that noxious brew?

Melitta Bentz, a housewife from Dresden, Germany, thought she could come up with a better way. She ripped a sheet of blotting paper out of her son's notebook, cut a circle of the porous paper, and stuck it in the bottom of a perforated brass pot. She reasoned that if she put the coffee grounds on top of this filter and poured the boiling water over it, she could extract the taste of the coffee without the bad side effects.

Melitta Bentz was right, and she was confident that more people than her husband, Hugo, would want to drink her filtered coffee. The couple hired a tinsmith to produce her newfangled pots for sale and in 1909 brought their drip system to the Leipzig Trade Fair. They sold twelve hundred of their "coffeemakers" that summer, and the Melitta company was born.

By 1912 Melitta was manufacturing its own line of coffee filters. The original disc was soon replaced with the familiar cone shape. Eventually the firm, run by Melitta Bentz's children and her children's children, would manufacture porcelain and plastic coffee pots and a full line of drip coffee accessories.

Today the Melitta system is used in more than 150 countries worldwide, and more than two-thirds of American coffee drinkers use the drip preparation method. And if they thought about it, any of them would happily start their day with a brief thank-you to a certain young Dresden coffee lover.

Anna Bissell
CARPET SWEEPER

Who invented the carpet sweeper? Game show contestants have been known to win money by answering Anna Bissell, and the preeminent brand of carpet sweeper certainly bears her name. And while we would love to report that indeed Anna Bissell did invent the Bissell sweeper, unfortunately it's not entirely true. Anna's husband, Melville Reuben Bissell, actually built the improved carpet sweeper still in use today.

However, it was Anna Bissell who saw the *need* for the Bissell sweeper. It was Anna who ran the Bissell company for many years after Melville's death, making her America's first female corporate executive officer—and making Bissell one of America's strongest corporations. And Anna did eventually invent a carpet sweeper herself: the Little Helper, a toy version of the famed household tool.

Anna and Melville Bissell were a young couple of solid New England stock when they moved to Grand Rapids, Michigan, in 1869. The family business was crockery, and every time Melville broke open a new box of dishes or glassware, it was Anna who had to contend with the sawdust and straw they came packed in. And Melville had allergies. . . .

There was already a carpet sweeper on the market in the 1870s, called the Welcome. In fact, the Bissells used to stock it in their retail store. But it just wasn't doing the trick. So Melville and Anna put together a better mousetrap, a carpet sweeper that utilized tufts of hog bristles (Anna hand-dipped the hog hair in tar) and was encased in a hand-tooled walnut case (Anna's idea). It was intended to—and did—effectively sweep up even the smallest particles from even the most uneven surfaces.

A patent application was filed on June 6, 1876; by 1881 the crockery shop served only as the lobby of a thriving carpet sweeper factory.

Anna herself would deliver materials to the Cedar Rapids piece-workers who made the brushes—"widows and other poor but respectable women," as a rule. The rapid growth of the Bissell Carpet Sweeper Company, later to become Bissell, Inc., was stalled more than once by tragedy. In 1884, the factory burned to the ground. In 1886 an entire line of defective sweepers had to be recalled. And worst of all, in 1889 Melville Bissell died of "black grippe" (probably pneumonia) at the age of forty-five.

There were five Bissell sons, but they were all too young to take over a corporation. It was expected that forty-two-year-old Anna would sell the company, or that one of the firm's aggressive salesmen would wrest control from her. Neither was the case. Anna Bissell continued to run the family company right through the 1920s, when she turned the reins over to her eldest boy. The Bissell corporation is still run by a Bissell heir today.

Anna Bissell was not only a strong woman, she was a marketing savant. She fiercely protected the Bissell trademark, to the point that "Bisselling" became common parlance for sweeping, especially in England. (Queen Victoria loved her Bissell!) Anna convinced a leery advertising department to put out brochures that lauded the sleek beauty of the sweeper and its exotic wood-trimmed case, rather than extolling its technical improvements. "Women don't care about machinery," she said. And as the sales figures reflected, she was right. It was Anna who didn't panic and convert the company to the vacuum cleaner business upon the advent of electricity; there would always be a niche for a lightweight picker-upper, she insisted. She was right again.

It's remarkable that the company still thrives—now a home care, health care, graphics, and, yes, carpet sweeper corporation exceeding $250 million in annual revenue. But it's even more remarkable that back in 1893 Anna Bissell was the first woman ever elected to the National Hardware Men's Association. And from 1923 until she died in 1934, at the age of seventy-seven, she was their chairman of the board.

Agnes McQueary
FABRIC SOFTENER SHEETS

True, it was Procter & Gamble chemist Conrad Gaiser who came up with the formula for Bounce brand heat-activated fabric-softener sheets. But it was nonchemist Agnes McQueary who made them actually work in the dryer.

When P&G was testing its new fabric softener sheets, it asked employees to bring their dirty laundry into the lab to be washed. And it was professional laundress McQueary who noticed the big problem with the product being tested: when the fabric softener sheet blocked the dryer's air vent, which was most of the time, the dryer overheated and shut itself off.

One night McQueary took some of the test sheets home with her and cut slits in them with a kitchen knife. She returned to the lab the next day and suggested the technicians try the sheets again.

The slits in the tissue let the air flow freely through the vent. The dryers didn't shut off. The fabric softener sheets were now marketable.

Procter & Gamble was unable to confirm whether or not Agnes McQueary got a cash bonus for her suggestion, but Susan Casey reports in *Women Invent* that she does hold a patent in her own name for the "improvement."

Jane Wells/Olivia Poole
JOLLY JUMPER

The first model of that nursery staple, the baby jumper, was patented in 1872 by Jane Wells of Chicago, Illinois. But the Jolly Jumper, that bright, bouncy brand-name version we still see everywhere, came a little later and from a little farther north. It was the brainchild of Olivia Poole, a mother of seven who grew up on the White Earth Reservation in Minnesota.

In the 1950s Poole combined Native American design with all-American ingenuity in an effort to keep her youngest child occupied. She suspended the cradle boards she had seen as a girl on the reservation from tree branches, using leather thongs. The contraption allowed a baby to touch the ground and bounce herself up and down—active, safe, and happily distracted.

Eventually Olivia and her husband, Joseph, fashioned the Jolly Jumper from fabric, elastic, and—to duplicate the bounce of a tree branch—a metal spring. It worked so well with her children that other mothers asked for one, too. Soon Olivia and Joseph moved to Canada to market the Jolly Jumper commercially. By 1959 their factory in Vancouver was producing several thousand Jolly Jumpers a month; they later sold the company for a significant profit. It's estimated that one out of every five Canadian babies grows up bouncing in a Jolly Jumper.

Laura Scudder
POTATO CHIPS IN BAGS

As the story goes, the potato chip was invented in 1853 by an ill-tempered cook named George Crum at Moon's Lake House in Saratoga Springs, New York. A customer complained that the fried potatoes were too thick and not crispy enough, so Crum went back to the kitchen and purposely overcooked the thinnest potato slices he could carve. He thought they'd be inedible. They were delicious.

But we can't credit the more than $3 billion potato chip business to Mr. Crum. That honor goes to the "Potato Chip Queen of the West": Laura Scudder of Monterey Park, California. It was Laura Scudder who first put potato chips in a waxed paper bag, making them a snack-food staple. It was Scudder's brainstorm to have home workers seal three sides of the bag with specially made irons. The bags were then filled at her factory, the fourth edge sealed, and the packets shipped to grocers.

It was quite an improvement over the original method of selling chips: scooping them out of a barrel. No one ever wanted the last third of the shipment!

When "the Potato Chip Queen of the West" tried to insure her delivery truck, she was turned down because she was a woman. (Courtesy of the Historical Society of Monterey Park)

Philadelphia-born Laura Scudder was already a successful businesswoman when she moved to Southern California and started her food company in 1926. In fact, she was the first female attorney in the town of Ukiah, California, having already worked as a nurse back east. It wasn't easy running a business during the Great Depression, though—especially not for a woman. When Scudder tried to get insurance for her one delivery truck, the insurance agents all turned her down. A woman couldn't be relied upon to pay the premiums, they said. Eventually Scudder found a female agent to write the policy—an agent who later got to insure the entire Scudder Foods fleet.

Scudder was a creative and loyal company owner. She helped Depression-era homemakers make ends meet by farming out the work of constructing those waxed paper bags. She also put a date on the bags, making Laura Scudder Foods the first company to freshness-date food products. And she turned down a $9 million offer to buy her firm, because the buyer wouldn't guarantee jobs for her existing employees.

Scudder was an iconoclastic and strong-willed woman, who not only broke precedent by running her own business but set tongues wagging when, after the death of her much-older husband, Charles, she married his son by a previous marriage, Charles Jr. That made her stepson her son's stepfather, a family dynamic that would befuddle even a soap opera writer.

By 1957, when Scudder did finally sell the company (for only $6 million, to a buyer who vowed to retain her workforce), Laura Scudder Potato Chips commanded 50 percent of the market in California. The company also sold peanut butter and Scudder's personal recipe for mayonnaise.

Laura Scudder died in 1959 at the age of seventy-eight, but her name and her reputation live on, in both grocery stores and a scholarship established in her name. In 1987, the food giant Borden bought Scudder Foods for an astounding $100 million.

Patsy Sherman
SCOTCHGARD

"Many of the world's greatest discoveries were unplanned," says chemist Patsy Sherman. "Penicillin. The vulcanization of rubber. They came about strictly by accident—but someone was keeping their eyes open and their brain in gear."

Sherman was certainly keeping her eyes open and her brain in gear that fateful day in 1952 at the research labs of the 3M Corporation. She was a new employee—a temporary employee, at that—with fresh bachelor's degrees in chemistry and mathematics. She was working in the exciting new field of fluorochemicals and polymerization, trying to come up with a sturdy synthetic rubber for aircraft hoses.

"We were not successful." Sherman sighs as she remembers. "The material tended to get stiff and brittle at cold temperatures. But while

It's easy to "spot" the Scotchgard-protected part of this tennis shoe. (Reproduced courtesy of 3M)

we were experimenting, someone in the lab spilled a sample of the new compound on her tennis shoes.

"When it dried, nothing could be found to remove it," remembers Sherman. "Soap wouldn't wet it. Solvent wouldn't wet it. We thought, 'Wouldn't it make a wonderful treatment for fabrics!'"

Sherman and her lab partner, Sam Smith, spent seven years testing and perfecting the stubborn substance before the Scotchgard line of fabric protectors was born. Sherman's name is first on the patent, and on sixteen others as well. She continued to work for 3M until her retirement in 1992 and was the first woman to be inducted into the company's honorary Carlton Society (1974) in recognition of her achievements. She later became the first woman named to the Minnesota Inventors Hall of Fame (1989) and was also invited onto the board of directors of the National Inventors Hall of Fame.

Not bad for a kid from Minnesota who, when she told her high school teacher she wanted to be a nuclear physicist, was named "most confused person" in the class. Sherman remembers the time she took her school's career-suitability test for girls: it told her to become a housewife. She insisted on taking the test they gave to boys: it said she was suited to be a chemist. Apparently the second test was more astute.

"Women are naturally inventive," says Sherman. "A woman can always find a dozen other uses for products besides what they were originally intended for." Her advice? "Don't ignore something that doesn't come out the way you expect it to. Keep looking at the world with inventor's eyes."

Joy Mangano
MIRACLE MOP

Sarah Boone never got rich from patenting the modern ironing board. Ellen Eglin made $18 for inventing the clothes wringer. Bertha Berman's fitted bedsheet didn't make her wealthy, nor did Penny Cooper's dehydrated food pouch, nor did Sally Raphael's mah-jongg coin-holder tray. So why has Joy Mangano become a multimillionaire by inventing a better mop?

Television.

In five years, Miracle Mop sales skyrocketed from $10,000 annually to $17 million annually. (Photo courtesy of Ingenious Designs, Inc.)

Mangano was a Long Island, New York, housewife in 1990, thirty-five years old and raising three young kids plus two older stepchildren, when she came up with the idea for a better mop. Five kids—this was definitely a woman who needed all the mop she could get. She called her self-wringing sensation the Miracle Mop, "the last mop you'll ever need." In 1991 she started a company in her bedroom, with one employee and a telephone. It racked up a tidy $10,000 in mop sales.

And then the QVC home-shopping channel featured the Miracle Mop on TV. By 1996, Mangano's Ingenious Designs, Inc., had two hundred employees in an eighty-thousand-square-foot manufacturing facility, and annual sales of close to $17 million.

Some 54 million American households saw Joy Mangano hawk her products on the direct-sales cable network. Millions more saw her display the Miracle Mop on half-hour infomercials, the bane or blessing of television advertising, depending on which side of the screen you sit on. Even in Europe, Asia, and the Caribbean, satellite-fed consumers have developed a voracious taste for home shopping.

Mangano, who has been inventing since she was a teenager (she says she came up with the idea of a fluorescent flea collar a year before the Hartz Mountain pet-food company put one on the market), has gone on to produce a bevy of practical products through Ingenious Designs. "Make Your Space a Better Place" is her slogan. There is the JewelKit, which stores jewelry; the Piatto Bakery Box, which stores cakes and cookies; and the RolyKit, which stores everything else. There is a Tuck-It Bucket for the mop and Replacemats for the table.

"I just love creating new products," says Mangano, who works seven days a week and manages to keep her family close by employing them.

Mangano, born and raised in suburban New York, earned a bachelor of business degree from Pace University. She later earned an Entrepreneur of the Year Award from Ernst and Young, and the Good Housekeeping Seal of Approval. But mostly she has earned the thanks of the Make-A-Wish Foundation (a portion of the proceeds from every sale is donated to the children's charity), the respect of her neighbors (all Ingenious Designs are manufactured in the United States), and the affection of her family. On her résumé, Joy Mangano lists her job qualifications as follows: Dynamic executive. Nurturing mother. Creative inventor. Contributor to quality.

Not a bad set of priorities for a TV pitchwoman.

Betty Cronin
TV DINNERS

When Betty Cronin patented the frozen TV dinner, there were two main stumbling blocks to the idea: One, most people didn't have television sets. And, two, most people didn't have freezers.

It was 1952. Swanson & Sons of Omaha, Nebraska, was a small, family-run business. Betty was a twenty-one-year-old bacteriologist, right out of college. Gilbert and Clark Swanson, the brothers who owned the company, were so excited about this new thing called TV that they figured people would want to watch it while doing anything and everything else. Including eating. "The question was," said Cronin, "what would people eat in their living rooms?"

The technical challenge, recalled Cronin, was "trying to come up with a dinner in which all the ingredients would require the same cooking time." Eventually she came up with the ubiquitous turkey, corn, and mashed potatoes—still the top-selling frozen dinner today. She sold her patent to the company for $1 ("I was an employee; it was my job"), and two years later the company sold itself to the Campbell Soup Company.

Betty Cronin spent her entire career perfecting the TV dinner, retiring as the director of Campbell's Microwave Institute in New Jersey.

Ruth Siems
STOVE TOP STUFFING

When General Foods sold its one-billionth box of Stove Top Stuffing in 1984—the first stuffing that could be made without needing actual poultry—they had T-shirts printed to commemorate the event. STUFF IT! said the shirt. "My feelings exactly," quipped Ruth Siems, the inventor of Stove Top. Apparently the company had neglected to send her a shirt.

While home economist Siems was just one of 850 scientists and cooks working at the General Foods technical center in the early 1970s developing laborsaving foods for all those newly working moms, it is her name that is listed first on the Stove Top patent. That's because it was she who solved the bread-crumb dilemma. The other researchers on her team were up to speed with chicken broth and dried onion, but only Siems could come up with the correct proportions and consistency for the bread crumbs.

For this contribution Siems was given a $25 bonus when the patent was filed, and a $100 bonus when the patent was granted. She also got a very nice plaque. General Foods went on to produce Stove Top Stuffing in chicken, turkey, cornbread, and pork flavors, in New England style and San Francisco style, in canisters and family-size boxes and made-for-the-microwave varieties. It is fair to say that their profits somewhat exceeded $125.

In 1985, when tobacco giant Philip Morris took over General Foods, Siems was unceremoniously laid off after thirty-three years of service.

Rose Totino

Frozen Pizza

The daughter of illiterate Italian immigrants, Rose Totino dropped out of high school to help support her six brothers and sisters, cleaning houses for $2.50 a week. In 1975 she sold her frozen-pizza line to Pillsbury Foods for $22 million. As rags to riches stories go, hers is a doozy.

When Rose married Jim Totino in 1934, there wasn't a lot of Italian cooking to be had in Minnesota. So they did it themselves. Rose began to bring her homemade pizza to PTA meetings, and the reception for this exotic foreign food was so warm that Rose and Jim opened a little restaurant.

They needed $1,500 to start the business and, as Rose put it, "we were $1,500 short." To obtain a loan, Rose walked into the bank with a portable oven and cooked up a pizza on the spot. It worked; she got the loan. Later, Rose would send representatives to supermarkets with portable ovens of their own, demonstrating her frozen-pizza line. That worked, too.

Totino's—still operating at 323 Central Avenue in Minneapolis—was a hit. After a while Rose got the idea that consumers nationwide would enjoy her pizza, if only there was a way to get it to them. Frozen foods were just finding a foothold in the American market, and the one brand of frozen pizza available tasted like cardboard. Rose perfected her frozen-pizza crust and got a patent for it. Soon, she and Jim were making pizzas in their living room, rotating the crust on a record player turntable and squirting on the sauce by hand. "The first day, we made seventy-five cases of pizza," recalled Rose in 1994.

Soon Totino Finer Foods gained distribution throughout the Midwest, then throughout the country. In 1975 Totino's was the top seller of frozen pizzas. By then, though, Jim Totino was ill with Parkinson's disease and Rose wanted out from under the burden of running the company. She sold Totino's to Pillsbury and became the first female vice president in that company's history.

Rose Totino was the first woman elected to the Frozen Food Hall of Fame but is best known in the Twin Cities as an ardent benefactress of education and religious radio. She died in 1994 at the age of seventy-nine, leaving children, grandchildren, great-grandchildren—and a brand name that lives on.

Elizabeth MacDonald
SPIC AND SPAN

Not only was Spic and Span the most popular cleaning product of its day, it was also the first cleaning product to be sold in grocery stores. Before that, cleansers were sold in hardware stores. Elizabeth MacDonald realized that women were doing the bulk of the cleaning, and women ran out to buy milk more often than they ran out to buy nails.

It was during the Great Depression in Saginaw, Michigan, that Elizabeth and her aunt, a chemist, concocted the super–sodium phosphate compound. It was patented in 1936, and Elizabeth and her husband, Glenn, started distribution: hardware stores, then grocery stores—even door to door. It was successful enough that soap giant Procter & Gamble bought them out in 1945.

MacDonald died in 1999 at the age of ninety-eight.

Helen Augusta Blanchard
ZIGZAG SEWING MACHINE

Some historical sources state that it was really Elias Howe's wife, Elizabeth, who invented the 1843 sewing machine with which he is credited. And there are sources claiming that Isaac Merritt Singer, who patented the sewing machine in 1851, was given more than just moral support by his (first) wife. But whether Mrs. Howe and Mrs. Singer are sewing-machine inventors unfairly overlooked by history, there is one woman sewing-machine inventor who *has* definitely been overlooked by history.

Helen Blanchard's zigzag sewing machine sits on display at the Smithsonian Institution in Washington, D.C. It's there because the innovation of the zigzag stitch, or "overseam," finally automated production of dry goods from silk scarves to wool blankets. The introduction of zigzag sewing is still usually credited to Singer, Necchi, or Pfaff—all of whom introduced the concept at a much later date. In fact, all of these sewing-machine companies purposely waited for Blanchard's 1873 patent to expire and then introduced their own zigzag models, because they didn't want to have to pay her royalties.

Helen Augusta Blanchard was a prolific inventor, with twenty-eight patents issued in her name between 1873 and 1915. Her inventions were all practical, commercial products and processes: zigzag sewing, surgical needles, hatmaking machines. Some of them, happily, did earn her significant royalties.

Born in Portland, Maine, Blanchard was the daughter of a wealthy shipbuilder. She invented mainly to earn money: when Dad died, the family went broke. A thrifty New Englander who never married, when she died in 1922, she had no children to leave her fortune to—nor anyone to protect her credits. Her sewing machine lives on, but her reputation died with her.

Caroline Garcin
AUTOMATIC SEWING MACHINE

According to historian Autumn Stanley, the earliest automatic sewing machine was designed by a Frenchwoman, Caroline Garcin. Indeed, she received an American patent for her development, and the thanks of the more hidebound bluestockings of her day. You see, the reason Mlle Garcin hired a clockmaker to build her spring-driven idea was to keep seamstresses from becoming sexually excited by foot-pedal sewing.

"The potentially nefarious masturbatory effects," as one physician put it, of treadle sewing machines on the French factory girls who sweated at them day after day was much cause for concern in the prudish 1860s. In fact, the "danger to women's health" was often used as an excuse to keep women from working.

The device must have been put to use, as Garcin and her co-inventor were honored by the French Academy of Sciences in 1872. No word on what the seamstresses thought.

Lillian Moller Gilbreth
STEP-ON TRASH CONTAINER

A trash can with a lid that opens when you step on a foot pedal, instead of your having to bend over and lift it up. A simple concept, but one that saves an enormous amount of back strain on a busy homemaker. Which is why Lillian Gilbreth, ergonomics pioneer and mother of twelve, thought it up.

A woman of prodigious energy, intellect, and compassion, Lillian Gilbreth was both scientist and supermom. No wonder they made a movie about her: it was Lillian Gilbreth who was portrayed by Myrna Loy in the classic film *Cheaper by the Dozen* (and its sequel, *Belles on Their Toes*).

After earning a master's degree in English from the University of California, young Lillian Moller was accepted into a doctoral program in 1903. But she took a lifelong detour when she met engineer Frank Gilbreth. One of the originators of the field of time-and-motion studies, Frank enchanted Lillian; they became partners in research and in life.

The pair had twelve children in seventeen years, and Lillian used their research to streamline home management as much from necessity as from scientific curiosity. The couple coauthored the groundbreaking book *Motion Study* in 1911, and, remarkably, Lillian went on to earn a doctorate in psychology and another in engineering while raising her outsize brood.

Lillian Gilbreth's path took another, sadder turn when Frank died in 1924. Although Lillian was officially the president of Gilbreth, Inc., the consulting firm the pair had founded in Montclair, New Jersey, she discovered that many clients would not deal with a woman. Money was tight. She continued to teach, however, as well as write, and in 1931 was the first recipient of the Gilbreth Medal—named after her late husband—awarded by the Society of Industrial Engineers.

Aside from the step-on trash-can lid and an improved electric can opener, Gilbreth's laborsaving contributions include refrigerator design (she came up with the egg-tray and butter-keeper concepts) and improvements to washing machines (the waste hose was her idea). She designed kitchens so that shelves, sinks, and tables were placed at the proper height for minimum fatigue. She went on to write three books of her own on scientific home management and pioneered the field of home design for the handicapped.

Gilbreth was the first woman elected to the National Academy of Engineering (1965) and the first woman to win the Hoover Medal for Distinguished Public Service (1966). In her lifetime she received more than twenty honorary degrees and special commendations; the Society of Women Engineers established a fellowship in her name.

A grandmother and great-grandmother many times over, Lillian Gilbreth wrote and lectured well into her eighties. She died in 1972 at the age of ninety-four. In 1984 the U.S. Post Office issued a stamp in her honor.

Virginia Holsinger
LACTAID

Lactaid, the milk-product digestive aid that is a lifesaver for the lactose intolerant, is a category buster. Should this enzyme supplement come in the chapter on medical innovations, somewhere after the medicine for gout, or in this chapter, with the frozen pizza? It is, after all, available in both the drugstore and the grocery store.

A coin toss from the editors lands Lactaid in here with the food-stuffs. A lifetime of research at the U.S. Department of Agriculture put Dr. Virginia Holsinger in a position to develop the profitable product.

Holsinger was among a group of dairy researchers approached by one Alan Kligerman, who was searching for a solution to the "nonspecific bowel complaint" (read: excess gas) produced in many adults by milk and milk products. The result of that work, Lactaid brand, now sells upwards of 3 million quarts a week.

It was also to Holsinger that Kligerman went when he sought a solution to a slightly *more* specific bowel complaint. That work led to the creation of the alpha-galactosidase product called Beano—the salvation of many a chili cook-off.

Dr. Holsinger retired in 1999 with forty-two years of USDA service and the unreserved thanks of the nation's ice cream lovers.

Sarah Cooper, Rose Markward Knox, Mary Wait
JELL-O

There's always room for Jell-O, as the advertising campaign goes—and, it seems, there's always room for another inventor of this popular gelatin dessert. From the time it was patented in 1845 to the time it was grossing seven-figure sales in 1906, gelatin desserts had been devised and improved by three separate couples.

As so often happens in history, it is the husbands whose names have been preserved. Now let us credit their partners.

The 1845 patent for clarified, fruit-flavored gelatin is held by Peter Cooper, the man who also designed and built America's first steam locomotive and, later, founded Cooper Union—the first free university for women and the working class.

To be fair and accurate, though, Peter Cooper only clarified the gelatin. Sarah Cooper added the color and fruit flavor.

In 1890 Charles and Rose Markward Knox started the Knox gelatin company, which still produces those orange boxes we see on grocery shelves today. It was Rose who prepared and tested all the recipes and popularized gelatin treats with her 1896 book *Dainty Desserts*.

After Charles died, Rose continued to run the Knox company almost up until her death at age ninety-two in 1950. A whirlwind of energy to the end, she was the first woman elected to the board of directors of the American Grocery Manufacturers' Association and always insisted on running the family business, in her words, "a woman's way."

The actual name "Jell-O" was coined in 1897 by one Mary Wait, wife of carpenter–turned–cough medicine manufacturer Pearl B. Wait. (Some accounts refer to the couple as Pearl and May Wait.) It was Mr. Wait who first commercially distributed the gelatin dessert mix—available in strawberry, raspberry, and orange flavors. Wait sold out for a pittance, however, to the Genessee Pure Food Company, and by 1906 Genessee was doing more than $1 million annually in sales.

Today Knox still produces gelatin, the Cooper Union still teaches, the Waits are a footnote in history—and more than 1 million packages of Kraft Foods' Jell-O are eaten every day.

And Let's Not Forget . . .

Sarah Boone, one of the most frequently named early African American inventors, improved the ironing board and received Patent #473,653 for it in 1892. Her very useful improvement was the narrow part you iron sleeves with. . . . **Nancy Johnson** patented the ice cream freezer in 1843. She sold the patent for $1,500, and one William G. Young—who patented his improved ice cream maker in 1848—gets textbook credit for the invention. But Johnson was first; before her mechanical freezer, you had to hand-stir with a spoon. . . .According to historian Charlotte Foltz Jones, peanut brittle was invented accidentally by a New England woman whose name is lost. Seems the woman got confused while making peanut taffy and used baking soda instead of cream of tartar. The result was rock hard—and delicious. . . . Delicious, creamy béchamel sauce, credited to Louis XIV courtier the marquis de Béchamel, was actually invented by his wife, the **marquise de Béchamel**. . . . the multimillion-dollar Pepperidge Farm company owes its success to **Margaret Rudkin**'s rough-textured whole-wheat bread . . . . Home economist **Jessie Cartwright** spent her career working for appliance manufacturers Norge and Bendix. She developed the delicate cycle for washing machines and the automatic ice-maker for refrigerators and is credited with early work on the Radarange microwave oven. . . . Two little boys and a tall husband inspired Californian **Rill Hall** to design the easy-to-clean Brease Toilet, for which she was awarded Design Patent #353,659 in 1994. . . . Film legend **Gloria Swanson** (yes, the one in *Sunset Boulevard*) turned inventor later in life; her company, Multiprises, holds her patent for a Dustless Broom, among other innovations. She later designed and marketed a line of clothing and cosmetics she called Forever Young. . . . The ubiquitous lazy Susan was patented in 1891 by **Elizabeth Howell** of Maryville, Missouri. She called it the "self-waiting table." . . . **Harriet Strong** not only patented the modern water storage dam, making her the "Walnut Queen of California," but also invented that clever pole-with-a-hook thing that you use to open transom windows. . . . The familiar needle threader was invented in 1901 by a fourteen-year-old girl named **Elena Popescu.** She never patented it, however, and so received neither credit nor income from the everyday device. . . . An anonymous woman at the 1904 Louisiana Purchase Exhibition fashioned the first ice cream cone out of the top waffle on her (melting) ice cream sandwich. . . . File under "Why didn't I think of that?": **Grace Petrini** was awarded Patent #4,797,952 in 1987 for the disposable Throwaway Bib. . . . A French housemaid whose name is lost to history accidentally invented dry cleaning in 1825. She spilled some turpentine on a tablecloth, and the more she tried to wipe away the evidence of her clumsiness, the cleaner the cloth became. . . . To keep us from going to the dry cleaners altogether, textile chemists **Ruth Benerito** and **Giuliana Tesoro** have done significant work on wash-and-wear fabrics. How significant? Dr. Benerito has more than fifty patents in her name; Dr. Tesoro boasts more than a hundred.

CHAPTER 3

Computer Liberation

W omen have always been on intimate terms with the computer. In fact, they helped to give birth to the computer revolution. Readers of *Mothers of Invention* will be familiar with Lady Ada Byron Lovelace, the nineteenth-century poet's daughter who co-developed the "analytical engine" and devised the first programming language. During World War II, a group of uncelebrated women operated and programmed the first modern-day computer.

A decade later, Rear Admiral Grace Murray Hopper, then only a lieutenant, solved a major obstacle in software through her invention of the automatic compiler, a device that precluded the need for re-inputting basic programs. That was about the same time Evelyn Berezin designed the first office computer and Betsy Ancker-Johnson was free-associating the groundwork of what would eventually become artificial intelligence.

In the 1970s Edna Schneider Hoover, a Bell Labs employee, had figured out a computerized solution to Ma Bell's biggest headache—equipment overload. By the end of the decade, women had laid the foundations for two vastly different aspects of computing: Roberta Williams launched "Mystery House," the world's first graphics-based computer game, while Lynn Conway invented the microchip that made supercomputers possible.

With such a rich legacy to call upon, it may shock some to hear that computer science classes are still dominated by male students in a four-to-one ratio. Conventional wisdom used to have it that men were simply more mathematical than women. Science has conclusively disproved this in the years since the ENIAC was created: research proves that women are actually better at converting an abstract concept into a tangible reality. This is because, thanks to a more complex structure, women use their left brain and right brain in tandem more efficiently than men do.

Why, then, the disparity in the number of male and female computer-science students? Could it be that the women who made modern computing a reality are not studied, or even acknowledged, in their textbooks? Denise Gurer, a computer scientist and noted historian of women in computing, observes that "often, in the past, a woman developed a new technology, then once the bugs had been worked out, the men moved in and took the credit.

"Imagine how things will change as this diminishes," says Gurer. "Men and women experience things differently. Given the chance, women will bring their different experiences to computing. Imagine what will happen then!"

Grace Murray Hopper
COBOL/COMPUTER COMPILER

There is a group of women engineers at Microsoft who call themselves the "Hoppers," and while reportedly a few of them can do a mean boogaloo, their name has nothing to do with their dance abilities. Rather, it's a tribute to Rear Admiral Grace Murray Hopper, who revolutionized computer software with her invention of the computer "compiler" in 1952. This was the first program to translate programming codes into language that could be read by computers.

Prior to Hopper's invention, computer programmers had to write time-consuming instructions for each new software package. "Why start from scratch with every single program you write? Develop one that would do a lot of the basic work over and over again," Hopper once said in an interview. "Nobody believed it could be done, yet it was so obvious. Developing a compiler was a logical move, but in matters like this, you don't run against logic—you run against people who can't change their minds."

COBOL isn't named for inventor Grace Murray Hopper, but the USS Hopper is. (Courtesy of the Naval Historical Center)

Hopper knew a lot about working for "people who can't change their minds." After all, she spent most of her adult life working for the U.S. Navy bureaucracy. In fact, when she retired at the rank of rear admiral in 1985—the first woman to earn that commission—she was the oldest person on active duty in the navy. This was the second time she retired. The first was in 1966, but within a year she was recalled to active duty. In this case the navy brass knew a good thing when they saw it and changed their mind to allow Hopper to oversee a program to standardize the navy's computer programs.

Born Grace Brewster Murray in New York City in 1906, Hopper came from an old navy family. Her great-grandfather—whom she recalls as a distinguished white-haired gentleman with muttonchop whiskers and a silver-topped walking cane—was Rear Admiral Alexander Wilson Russell, who served in the Civil War.

She was remembered as a curious child. Once, when she was seven, her curiosity led her to dismantle an alarm clock in an effort to see how it worked. By the time her mother figured out what was occupying her eldest child, Grace had gone through seven clocks in the house. Thereafter she was restricted to only one clock.

Both her parents encouraged Grace to pursue her educational ambitions. By the time she was sixteen, she was ready to attend Vassar College but had to delay her plans when she unexpectedly flunked a Latin exam. Finally entering Vassar a year later, she graduated in 1928. At age twenty-three, Grace married Vincent Foster Hopper, a bright young English scholar who had just graduated with highest honors from Princeton and was teaching at New York University School of Commerce. Grace pursued her education at Yale for graduate studies, where she received her Ph.D. in mathematics, eventually returning to Vassar to teach.

When Pearl Harbor was bombed in 1941, Grace immediately wanted to serve her country by joining the navy, but the military officials politely said no. At thirty-four, she was considered too old to enlist—plus, she was sixteen pounds underweight for her height of five feet six inches, according to navy standards. Furthermore, the government declared her occupation as a mathematics professor crucial, and she was told she could best serve the war effort by remaining a civilian. Undaunted, she wangled special dispensation (undoubtedly through family connections) and was sworn into the U.S. Naval Reserve in 1943.

Lieutenant Hopper was assigned to the Bureau of Ordnance Computation Project at Harvard University, where she worked as a programmer on a calculating device called the Mark I, a precursor to electronic computers. In fact, she was the third person ever to program it.

Following the war she found herself divorced (though she would keep her married name) and, one year later, out of a navy job (though she maintained her career as a naval reservist). She became a senior programmer with Remington Rand, where she worked on UNIVAC, the first large-scale commercial computer. She was director of automatic programming at Sperry Corporation when she published her first paper on computer compilers, and she is credited with leading the team that developed COBOL, the first user-friendly business computer software program, which is still widely used today.

Defiantly independent, the chain-smoking Hopper once commented that "it was easier to ask for forgiveness than permission." In her office hung a clock that ran counterclockwise, a way of reminding visitors that just because something always has been done a certain way doesn't mean it can't be done another way.

Initially Hopper received faint praise for her innovations. Her response was to quip, "If you do something once, people will call it an accident. If you do it twice, they call it a coincidence. But do it a third time and you've just proven a natural law." However, in September 1991 President George Bush awarded her the National Medal of Technology "for her pioneering accomplishments in the development of computer technology and opening the door to a significantly larger universe."

Hopper is the first woman to receive this prestigious award, the nation's highest honor in engineering and technology. By the time she died on January 1, 1992, Hopper had received honorary degrees from thirty universities and numerous other awards, had been inducted into the National Women's Hall of Fame, and was even the first recipient of the "Man of the Year" award from the Data Processing Management Association.

Perhaps her greatest honor—one that her great-grandfather no doubt would be proudest of—was the commissioning of a U.S. Navy ship in her name in 1996. The destroyer USS *Hopper* is a 466-foot, 8,300-ton technological marvel filled with advanced computer-controlled equipment. As is the tradition, the ship bears its own coat of arms whose motto reads "Dare and Do," a phrase Rear Admiral Hopper frequently used in issuing advice.

Roberta Williams
COMPUTER GAMING

Before Roberta Williams came onto the scene, computer games consisted of funny little blobs that ate other funny blobs. In the late seventies that was considered technical innovation. But Williams thought that this completely underutilized the medium. Why couldn't computer entertainment be fun and intelligent? The answer to that

*Roberta Williams
created the world's
first graphics-based
computer game.
(Courtesy of Ken
Williams)*

question led her to create a whole new industry and establish a company that is today the largest worldwide publisher of interactive entertainment and educational software.

Roberta's gigantic and successful enterprise, Sierra On-Line, began humbly in 1979 on a kitchen table in her home. Her husband, Ken, eager to create a FORTRAN compiler for Apple computers, wanted to buy an early Apple II. Roberta wasn't pleased with the prospect. "That machine represented several mortgage payments for the house," she remembers. To placate her and to interest her in computers, Ken brought home a text-based adventure game with his new computer. While Ken toiled away writing "serious software," Roberta puzzled her way through the game, finishing it with a sense of exhilaration and a heavy dose of computer game addiction.

Disappointed with the other text adventure games available at the time, Roberta mapped out her own game and presented Ken with a stack of papers containing the script, maps, and puzzles for her idea. It was an entirely different kind of game, with characters and a plotline in which the player was given choices.

To make her project appeal to Ken, who at that time thought of computers as serious machines meant only for solving serious problems, Roberta suggested that they include pictures. A computer that makes pictures? Now, *that* was a serious challenge. Ken created the tools to produce the game art, programmed the logic for the game, and devised a way to cram seventy pictures on a disk (keep in mind that this was way back in 1979; the process the Williamses developed for including pictures was revolutionary), while Roberta wrote the text and designed the art.

The result was "Mystery House," the world's first graphics-based computer game and the beginning of Roberta's career as a game designer. Within ten months of its release in 1980, it sold fifteen thousand copies and grossed an astonishing $167,000—unheard-of figures at the dawn of computer gaming. "Designing a game was much different then," says Roberta. "The role of the designer has changed so much. In those days a designer was a writer, artist, director, producer, and editor. We were 'hands-on' to the end. We managed the project from the concept through quality assurance."

Today her company, headquartered in Bellevue, Washington, employs over seven hundred people. Williams holds the personal distinction of authoring and designing more home-computer games than any other person in the gaming industry.

From the beginning she has been committed to creative game design. In 1982 she collaborated with Muppets creator Jim Henson to design a computer-adventure game based on his feature fantasy *The Dark Crystal*. The game was a critical and commercial success. She had equal success with the King's Quest saga, based on the legend of Camelot. The first episode, "King's Quest I: Quest for the Crown," released in the summer of 1984, was the first 3-D animated adventure game.

In 1987 Williams released her first children's title, "Mixed-Up Mother Goose." As a mother of two children, she felt that the time had come to appeal to younger players. Five awards, two hundred thousand units, and eight years later, this innovative title lives on in 1995's updated and graphically sophisticated "Mixed-Up Mother Goose Deluxe."

"King's Quest IV" in 1989 was the first game to contain VGA graphics and take full advantage of the new music-card technology with a fully orchestrated stereo soundtrack. This award-winning game was also significant in that it featured a female protagonist. "King's Quest VII: The Princeless Bride" went one better, telling the tale of a mother and daughter caught in an enchanted world.

More than 3 million copies of the King's Quest series have been sold, making Williams the bestselling game designer in the industry.

In the nineties, Williams once again pushed the electronic-gaming envelope with ultrarealistic 3D-rendered backgrounds. Both 1995's "Phantasmagoria" and 1997's "King's Quest: Mask of Eternity" employed Sierra On-Line's proprietary ThreeSpace3D game engine.

"I hate to call what I do 'games,'" says Williams. "I think of them more as interactive stories. Every story has to be well written and engaging, but it's up to the designer to add the interactivity—the roundness of exploration and the challenge of the puzzles."

Ada Byron, Lady Lovelace
FIRST COMPUTER LANGUAGE

There's no little irony that the father of the early-nineteenth-century English literary movement known as romanticism was also the father of the inventor of the first computer language. Lord Byron embodied the concept of the brooding poet, all Sturm und Drang in addition to being a genius of letters. He even died mysteriously in a storm at the tragically young age of thirty-six.

His daughter, Augusta Ada Byron, would inherit much of the dramatic inclinations that characterized his life. But Ada, as she was known, also possessed a precise mathematical mind. The combination of science and imagination laid not only the foundation for her ability to write the first computer language but also to her correctly predicting the future of computing.

While her father's genius is often given credit for Ada's prescient mind, it was actually her mother, Lady Byron, who provided the inspiration for her to pursue computing. Five weeks after Ada was born, Lady Byron asked for a separation from her husband and was awarded sole custody of the baby. Terrified that Ada might follow in her father's calamitous footsteps, Lady Byron brought her up to be a scientist and mathematician, a decidedly odd education for a young lady of the aristocracy.

Despite her mother's best intentions, Ada did not completely sublimate her poetical leanings. As Yale University's Dr. Betty Toole wrote in her essay "Women in Computing," Ada's "understanding of mathematics was laced with imagination, and described in metaphors." She announced to her mother at one point in her education that she hoped to be "an analyst and a metaphysician" and once wrote to her, "if you can't give me poetry, can't you give me poetical science?"

In addition to her mother, Ada was influenced in her education by writer Mary Somerville. She encouraged Ada to pursue her mathematical studies and introduced her to her wide circle of friends. It was at one of her dinner parties, in 1834, that Ada first learned of Charles Babbage and his idea for a new calculating device, which he called the Analytical Engine. Babbage suggested that a machine might be built that not only could foresee the answer to an analytical problem by could actually act upon it. Ada was immediately charmed by the "universality of his ideas."

In autumn of 1841 Babbage drew plans for this new engine, which was reported on by a French scientific publication. Ada translated the article and showed it to Babbage, with whom she was now acquainted through her husband, the Earl of Lovelace. Babbage knew of Ada's pursuit of science and mathematics and suggested she add her own thoughts to the article before he published it in English. She accepted the invitation and expanded the article by three times its original length.

In her article, published in 1843, Ada correctly predicted that such an analytical machine might be used to compose music, produce graphics, and perform both personal and scientific tasks. She particularly outlined how the engine might calculate numerical probability. This plan is now widely regarded as the first computer program. (In 1979 the U.S. Department of Defense would name a sophisticated software "Ada" in honor of her achievement.)

In one of the most famous passages from the article, Ada anticipated the debate about whether computers would ever have the capacity to acquire so-called artificial intelligence. She cautioned that "it is desirable to guard against the possibility of exaggerated ideas that might arise as to the powers of the Analytical Engine [which] . . . has no pretensions whatever to originate any thing."

Nevertheless, the machine's "distinctive characteristic" to create and store programs for reuse, she wrote, was likely to have a profound "influence on science itself." By "so distributing and combining the truths and the formulae of analysis, that they may become most easily and rapidly amenable to the mechanical combinations of the engine, the relations and the nature of many subjects in that science are necessarily thrown in to new lights, and more profoundly investigated."

Her prediction was right on the mark, as computers have made possible everything from space travel to mapping the human genome. The fortunate side of Lord Byron's indelible influence on his daughter was her genius. The unfortunate side was her impetuosity. A mother of three, she scandalized London society with her numerous love affairs, and shortly after the publication of her article, gambled away the family fortune. Soon after, she developed chronic asthma, and then finally succumbed to uterine cancer. Like her father, she died tragically young at age thirty-six.

Lynn Hershman Leeson
VIRTUAL FILM SET

Filmmaker Lynn Hershman Leeson was smitten the first time she learned about Ada Byron. "I knew instantly I had to make a film about her. This daring and brilliant woman of Victorian era not only predicted the possibilities of artificial life but also the digital revolution that happened a hundred forty-four years after her death."

Leeson's fascination and resolve became *Conceiving Ada,* a feature film that was screened in 1997 at the Sundance Film Festival, the most prestigious of U.S. film showcases. Even more interesting was that *Conceiving Ada* marked the debut of Leeson's "virtual sets," an innovative digital technology she invented that promises to revolutionize film production.

"Because the crowning glory of Ada Byron was to create the first computer language, it seemed fitting that a digital process be used to tell her story," says Leeson. Her new technique allows background still images to be dynamically placed into live video. Prior to shooting, the still images are digitized, altered, colorized, and made into mattes. (A matte is a motion-picture effect in which part of a scene is blocked out and later replaced by footage from another source.) On the set the actors perform against blank walls while monitors show them in their virtual environment.

In the past, creating such effects was a laborious process reserved for postproduction. This denied the actors the luxury of responding to their surroundings. The director had to instruct the actor to pretend, for example, that a very large lizard was about to step on him. With Leeson's invention, actors can actually see their virtual props and background scenery.

"The immediacy of shooting live action while simultaneously manipulating digitized background in real time was exhilarating for the actors," says Leeson. "They found their reactions becoming more spontaneous and their relationship to the otherwise totally blue [screen] environment much more interactive."

To create the process, Leeson used various existing computer programs, such as Photoshop and Quicktime. More than 385 separate photographs and mini-movies were numbered and scanned into the computer. Thus, when the scene called for people to walk through nonexistent doors or for make-believe rain to fall on invisible windows, Leeson and her crew could just punch in a number and—voilà!—instant scenery.

While *Conceiving Ada* was Leeson's first feature film, she has produced more than seventy major short and full-length video works and is an internationally recognized interactive and video artist. Her work has been shown in over two hundred exhibitions in museums and galleries worldwide and is included in such collections as those of the Museum of Modern Art in New York and the Seattle Art Museum.

In *Conceiving Ada*, the fictional protagonist, Emmy Coer, is an artificial-life researcher obsessed with Ada Byron. She finds a way to digitally channel Ada's spirit, virtually experiencing her life—just as Leeson virtually created a movie set. "I felt it important to use the technology Ada pioneered, because it provided another dimension through which to tell her story," says Leeson. "The use of virtual sets and digital sound became environments through which Ada becomes liberated and ultimately moves freely through time."

Nancy Burson
THE AGING MACHINE

By now most of us are familiar with "morphing," the computer process by which faces and objects meld into different images. Filmmaker James Cameron brought morphing to new heights in his film *Terminator 2* in 1991, while recording artist Peter Gabriel employed the technique in groundbreaking music videos a decade earlier. But the idea and its first application originated with artist and photographer Nancy Burson, who conceptualized the process in 1969 and eventually patented it to create "an aging machine."

"I had an idea to build an interactive device that could show how people would look as they aged. People's faces generally age in the same way. If you could map those areas and use that as a type of template over an individual's photograph, you could essentially see how they looked ten or twenty years in the future," she said.

Unfortunately, she had to wait for computer technology to catch up with her idea. By the late 1970s, however, a group of MIT programmers were anxious to show off their latest hardware, and with their help she designed her prototype aging machine. The project was a curious collaboration of computer engineers and an avant garde artist, and one of the first, she notes, in which "a computer interfaced with a human face."

Burson went on to refine the software, and in 1981 she patented the technology under the name Face Software.

As an artist, Burson was primarily interested in the technology as a vehicle for her lifelong exploration of the human face. But there was one very practical use for her fast-forward faces: law enforcement could use them to identify missing children or criminals, years after they had disappeared. When the FBI came to Burson in 1988, she rose to the occasion.

Since the photographs had to be accurate to be useful, Burson needed to modify the process somewhat. Photographs of relatives of the missing person were scanned and then digitized, in order to establish how each particular facial structure aged. Even so, there was considerable question as to whether the process could actually predict how a child missing since he was four might actually look ten years later.

Within the first year of its use, Burson's aging machine was responsible for finding three missing children and over the years has aided in finding dozens more. "Many of these children were in abusive situations, so it was very gratifying to be able to help."

The New York artist continues to be exhibited by major galleries and museums around the country, and she considers her role as an inventor secondary. Indeed, in a recent exhibition of photography in a Manhattan gallery she abandoned the morphing process altogether, focusing rather on portraits of children and adults she has befriended who have "devastating facial anomalies resulting from surgery, cancer, or congenital defects."

In this sense Burson's latest work is a continuation of her twenty-year quest to question what we perceive as normal or beautiful. "Picasso was the original morpher," she says, smiling.

In different hands Burson's technology might heave been exploited far more commercially. One can imagine aging machines in malls, in plastic surgeons' offices, and at every Hollywood special-effects company. In fact, Burson admits that she allowed her original patent, on which she spent $35,000, to lapse. And while she initially sold her Face Software to law enforcement agencies, Burson wouldn't accept any payment from the National Center for Missing and Exploited Children. Though she cannot claim to have made a fortune from her invention, the conversations she's had with parents of missing children whom she's helped to find are priceless. "There's absolutely nothing better."

Portia Isaacson

HIGH-TECH HOME (AND MOTOR HOME)

When the phone rings, all radios and television sets are instantly muted. Before leaving work, you can call your house and instruct it to draw a bath that will be ready upon your arrival. A repairperson may enter when no one is at home by using a temporary code, and if she goes into an "off-limits" area, she will be warned to leave. If she does not, the homeowner and the police will be notified.

These are just a few features of the Intellihome, a futuristic house in Dallas, Texas, designed by computer scientist and entrepreneur

Portia Isaacson in 1986. And what a house! The six thousand-square-foot white stucco Bauhaus-like structure featured black marble floors, recessed lighting, and walls of tempered glass. But it was the guts of the house that made it unique. Eight miles of wiring—hidden discreetly behind custom cabinetry—thirteen computers, twenty video monitors, and sixteen telephones together created the best command center outside of the Pentagon.

As well as quieting phones and filling tubs, Intellihome could monitor the whereabouts of family members, greet visitors using a robot, and send images from outside via remote-controlled cameras onto any TV monitor in the home. It even came complete with a built-in anti-hacking system.

The first of its kind, this fit-for-the-Jetsons residence was not cheap. The electronics alone added another half million dollars to the $600,000 building cost. Isaacson financed it through a windfall profit she made when she sold her company to McGraw-Hill for a cool $48 million.

"I have had lots of friends who sold companies and got a lot of money, using it to buy a yacht, an airplane, a year's trip around the world," she recalls. "We used our money to build the house."

While the house was customized, the actual electronic components were strictly off the shelf. That feature interested manufacturers, and soon Sony, Panasonic, IBM, and AT&T were giving Isaacson their latest equipment to showcase. Intellihome appealed to these companies because the house looked appealing. "My goal was to prove that technology doesn't have to be ugly," says Isaacson. "We wanted nothing less than a platform for presenting technology as a form of sculpture."

Isaacson, the first person in her Oklahoma dairy family to attend high school, idolized Marie Curie and from the age of four knew she wanted to be a scientist. Married and in college at twenty-one, she was left with three small boys when her husband abandoned the family. She remarried, earned a Ph.D. in physics from Southern Methodist University, and then founded, ran, and later sold Future Computing.

Today Isaacson is a leading consultant on emerging technologies and the author of several hundred articles on the subject. Aspects of her home design have been borrowed over the years by various builders, but as yet no farsighted contractor has taken the plunge and built a whole Intellihome. Isaacson still has hope.

In the meantime she's taken Intellihome's technology and incorporated it into a high-tech motor home with multiple computers, satellite television and a home theater system. She calls it Thunder TeePee and is in discussion now with RV manufacturers.

In a recent article Isaacson wrote about the potential of computer technology. "Digital's power to change our world is not comparable to the printing press [nor] . . . steam engine. It is more. Perhaps 1,000 years from now, as the year 3000 approaches, the discovery of digital will be viewed as having been comparable to the emergence of intelligence or language, but surely nothing less."

Evelyn Berezin
OFFICE COMPUTER,
AIRLINE RESERVATIONS SYSTEM

About the same time that Texas secretary Bette Nesmith Graham was coming up with the idea for Liquid Paper, physics Ph.D. Evelyn Berezin was approaching the creation of error-free data processing from an entirely different perspective. While working for typewriter manufacturer Underwood in 1953, she designed the first office computer, but because Underwood was bought out by a competitor, Olivetti, the innovation was never marketed.

Undaunted, Berezin went on to design the first nationwide airline computer reservations system, which was used by United Airlines in sixty cities for eleven years. Still later she formed her own company, Redactron, where Berezin and colleague Ed Wolf designed the Data Secretary, a machine that improved significantly on IBM's editing typewriter and came much closer to what we now expect from word-processing technology.

Berezin sold Redactron in 1976 and pursued a career in investment management. Today she is president of Greenhouse Management Corporation and a director for several other firms.

Alicia Page
LIBRARY DATABASE

Librarian Alicia Page from Avon, Massachusetts, was frustrated at work. In 1978 interlibrary loans took six months and involved a painstaking search by phone or mail of each library. Page was also frustrated at home. At fifty-seven, she was recently divorced and broke. But Alicia Page had an idea. "Wouldn't it be interesting," she thought, "if I could put all of the South Shore Library holdings on one database, put a CRT in each library, and make the librarians feel like they're big computer operators?" That's just what she did, and the result was that librarians could do an instant search of all the local libraries for any title. Page sold her house and used the money to start her own company, Computer Engineering Associates, which by 1985 was doing over $6 million in sales annually.

Caroline Fu
WORKSTATION FOR THE HANDICAPPED

Caroline Fu devised a voice-controlled computer workstation for the disabled while working at Boeing Computer Services' Artificial Intelligence Center. The workstation features two robotic arms for such tasks as inserting diskettes. It was tested by a quadriplegic programmer and reportedly enables a disabled worker to be "completely vocationally independent." Fu's workstation may have additional applications—for example, to be used by nonimpaired workers while their hands are otherwise occupied. Fu's invention is also under consideration for use in space.

Shaula Alexander Yemini
COMPUTER NETWORK DEBUGGER

The legend goes that Grace Murray Hopper, the inventor of the computer compiler and COBOL, also coined the term "computer bug" when she found a large moth jamming the inner workings of an early prototype computer. So it's only fitting that a woman invented a system for eliminating the digital bugs that creep into today's sophisticated computer networks.

Anyone who uses a network workstation or ties into an intranet knows the havoc that ensues when the system is "down." "Right now what happens if the system crashes is that someone has to go through logs and logs of data to figure out what went wrong," says Dr. Shaula Yemini, president of System Management Arts in White Plains, New York. This can take a long time, and companies can lose a lot of money. One minute of downtime for a brokerage firm, for instance, can cost as much as $100,000.

In 1998 Dr. Yemini devised a program called SMARTS that will do the task of analyzing the system automatically, quickly, and accurately. Essentially the software tool identifies the cause of the problem from the cascade of symptoms it causes. Up to 80 percent of network downtime is spent searching for the root cause of a fault, a classic case of I-could-fix-it-if-only-I-could-find-it. SMARTS allows a systems operator to find "it" in seconds.

The technology has been endorsed by some heavy hitters in the computer industry, including Hewlett-Packard, the world's largest producer of network and systems-management products. Motorola Satellite Communications used the technology while building the Iridium Project, a worldwide satellite-communications system.

Rachel Zimmerman
Blissymbol Program

As a project for her school science fair, twelve-year-old Rachel Zimmerman created a computer program with pictorial symbols that allow for nonverbal communication. The "speaker" communicates by pointing to the different symbols—Blissymbols, as Rachel called them—on a page or board. The user touches the symbols on a touch-sensitive board or screen, and the program translates them into written language. Thus the user can record thoughts or communicate over distance via e-mail. Rachel won the YTV Achievement Award for

Innovation—given by a Canadian children's television network—for her invention. Currently her program translates into English and French, and Hebrew will be available soon.

While the Blissymbol Printer has allowed her to travel around the world to demonstrate her invention at various science fairs, Rachel is not resting on her laurels. Upcoming projects include "Disposal of Domestic Nuclear Waste" and "Clean, Green Power: Light to Electricity Through Photosynthesis of Algae."

Susan Kasen Summer, Shin-Yee Lu, Elizabeth Downing
3-D INNOVATIONS

One of the imaginary devices that captured the public's attention in the original *Star Wars* movie was the 360-degree, holographic three-dimensional image. (Remember when Princess Leia first made her appeal to Luke Skywalker?) Three women working separately have created inventions that are bringing that product of filmmaker George Lucas's imagination very close to reality.

Susan Kasen Summer wasn't satisfied with the quality of the three-dimensional graphics software available for personal computers. The fixed hologram images looked flat, due largely to the limitations of flat computer screens. So she invented "high definition volumetric display," or HDVD, which creates the illusion of a three-dimensional object suspended in the air a few feet in front of a specially designed screen. "The images appear so real that they defy the brain's ability to perceive them as virtual," she says. What's more, the 3-D effect can be achieved with moving images. She envisions 3-D moving billboards, à la *Blade Runner*, which utilize her HDVD technology.

Shin-Yee Lu, a Lawrence Livermore National Laboratory engineer, approached the problem of moving 3-D images from another . . . well, angle. While working on a way to assist robots to grasp and manipulate objets, she got the idea of exploiting the different textures on an object in the robot's video-camera eyes. (This task comes naturally to humans, because each eye scans an object from a slightly different angle while the brain integrates the two images.) Her video-stereoscopic technology worked so well that soon lab robots were performing the most exacting task: handling nuclear waste. And it's now being used to make computerized 3-D images for everything from virtual-reality software to face-recognition security systems.

As Susan Kasen Summer noted, the illusion of 3-D images depends on tricking the eye and brain into believing that one or more two-dimensional images are really solid objects. Elizabeth Downing thought that the better way was to replicate how television creates images, through individual pixels. Atoms of certain rare elements will absorb two slightly different colors of invisible infrared light and convert the energy into visible light. By confining these elements to a glass cube and then sweeping them with beams of infrared light, the human eye perceives these points of light as three-dimensional objects. In 1995 Downing formed 3-D Technology Laboratory to commercialize the technology, which she hopes to use for medical imaging, air traffic control, radar, and anything else that might benefit from precise 3-D imaging. (How about a movie theater in the round with the film being shown inside a 3-D cube?)

All three women were honored individually for their 3-D innovations by *Discover* magazine's prestigious Discover Awards.

Edith Clarke, Edna Schneider Hoover
UTILITY EQUIPMENT

While women have excelled in all areas of computer software, they haven't shied away from tackling hardware problems, either. Two examples are Edith Clarke (1883–1959), an electrical engineer who created a "graphical calculator" that solved a major problem with electric power-transmission lines, and Edna Schneider Hoover, a Bell Labs researcher who created a computerized switching system for telephone-call traffic.

Born in a small farming community in Maryland, Clarke attended Vassar College and taught mathematics before enrolling as a civil-engineering student at the University of Wisconsin in 1911. At the end of her first year she took a summer job as a "computer assistant" at

AT&T, and became so enthralled with the work that she did not return to her studies.

Clarke went on to become the first woman to earn an electrical-engineering degree from MIT and then accepted a job with General Electric. Two years later, in 1921, she filed a patent for her device, and the timing could not have been better. Power systems were becoming increasingly complex, and her "graphical calculator" allowed engineers to translate esoteric mathematical methods into graphs.

Hoover was a Ph.D. in mathematics from Yale University. It was while in the hospital after giving birth to one of three daughters that she sketched the design for her patented computerized telephone-switching system. The invention would earn her one of the first software patents, #3,623,007, awarded on November 23, 1971. The principles of her switching systems are still widely used today.

At the time Bell Labs was being overwhelmed with the exponential growth in telephone traffic. There was dire need to replace their hard-wired and mechanical switching equipment with a more efficient system. Hoover's invention used a computer to monitor the volume of incoming calls periodically and adjust the call-acceptance rate accordingly, thus eliminating the danger of equipment overload.

Lynn Conway

SUPERCOMPUTER AND MICROELECTRONICS CHIP DESIGN

> *In Virginia Woolf's novel* Orlando, *the eponymous main character awakens as a woman, previously a man, sees her image in the mirror and reflects:*
>
> *"Same person, no different at all—just a different sex."*

A great mind transcends gender. And from Lynn Conway's brilliant mind came significant contributions in engineering and computing, which have paved the way for computing as we know it today. She has recently retired from a prestigious career in engineering and academia and enjoys an active outdoor lifestyle with her boyfriend of thirteen

Lynn Conway's ingenuity paved the way for today's supercomputers. (Courtesy of Lynn Conway)

years. She has worked on secret computer and Department of Defense projects. But it was her personal secret that was too devastating to share. Lynn Conway was born a boy.

The question of gender identity has been explored and debated. What does it mean to be born a man or a woman? Does one's gender identity reside in the chemical makeup of the body, the mind, or the soul? Are our gender-associated behaviors learned or innate? Are boys and girls encouraged to excel in different subjects? Are we spirits trapped in social constructs called masculinity and femininity? Do our spirits feel more comfortable in one shell versus another?

When Lynn Conway was born Robert Sanders (a pseudonym she has adopted to protect her family) to middle-class parents—a school-teacher and a chemical engineer—in Mount Vernon, New York, during the 1940s, there were signs at a young age that Robert was not an average male. He asked to wear dresses and preferred the company and activities of young girls to those of young boys. The question of gender was not a topic for discussion; rather, his "feminine" behaviors were repressed by his parents.

The one refuge Robert found was in exploring science and nature with his brother. Together they scavenged for refuse material to turn into projects—scrap lumber, galvanized tin, and aluminum. His talent for design and construction produced many creations: a hi-fi system, a wood-framed photo enlarger, even a radio telescope. This determination and drive would remain a constant throughout his life.

Liberated from his parents at MIT, Robert began to experiment with hormones and assert his feminine persona, Lynn, a derivation of his middle name. Robert excelled academically, but his personal turmoil and conflict were taking their toll. He contacted doctors hoping to learn more about transsexuality and surgery options, only to be discouraged. Faced with the unbearable prospect of living the gender role assigned to him, Robert hit rock bottom and dropped out of MIT.

After a succession of menial jobs, Robert craved intellectual challenge and enrolled in 1961 at Columbia University where he excelled, earning bachelor's and master's degrees in electrical engineering after only two years. His outstanding performance garnered attention at IBM, and he was offered a job.

At IBM Robert worked on a secret supercomputer project. He invented a method for a single processing unit (CPU) to perform multiple operations simultaneously. This breakthrough, known as "dynamic instruction scheduling," or DIS, was a way of constantly analyzing a string of instructions and ordering them efficiently while keeping the number of transistors performing these logical tests to a minimum. DIS is a key method for speeding up modern processing chips, including the Intel Pentium.

However, professional achievements could not reconcile the turmoil Robert Sanders was experiencing internally. Still trying to fit the masculine role assigned to him, he married a young woman and fathered two girls. Hiding his true persona, he plunged into married life and seemed to accept nature's terrible mistake. But eventually this suppression of his true nature led Robert to a boiling point. Almost suicidal, he contacted Dr. Harry Benjamin, an expert on transsexualism. Dr. Benjamin, near retirement, agreed to take him on as one of his last patients, and Robert resumed estrogen therapy and prepared for a sex-change operation.

This was a decision that cost him his friends, his family, and his job. However, there simply was no other option.

Flying solo, through sheer will and determination, Lynn Conway was able to find a programming job at Memorex, without being able to leverage her education or her groundbreaking work at IBM. She began a phase of her life she refers to as "deep stealth mode." However, by 1971 Conway was living a full life. The liberation that sex-reassignment surgery afforded her renewed her energy and her passion for her work, and by 1973 her successes garnered attention at Xerox's exciting and innovative Palo Alto Research Center (PARC).

While at PARC, Conway forged her most significant contribution to the computing industry and flourished both as a woman and as an engineer. There she met Carver Mead, a semiconductor researcher at the California Institute of Technology. At the time the architects of the chip did not understand microelectronics—Conway did and realized the need to simplify chip design. Conway invented scalable design rules that greatly simplified chip layout. Then, together, Mead and Conway reconceptualized the entire chip-design process for the new technology of very large-scale integrated circuits, or VLSI. They slimmed an enormous range of logic and circuit design styles into a single basic methodology that could be quickly and easily learned by computer engineers.

Conway knew they had "hit the mother lode," she says. "But what do you do with this new method in order to make it legitimate?" In 1979 Mead and Conway disseminated their work in a textbook, complete with examples, called *Introduction to VLSI Systems*, or as it became known to a generation of engineering students, "Mead-Conway."

Hired back by MIT, she was not quite sure what to expect, having kept her previous attendance there a secret. Nervous about teaching the course, she overprepared, and her meticulous notes became the instructors' guide for the first modern VLSI course. Further cementing the legitimacy of the new VLSI design rules, Conway quickly implemented the student chip-design projects, with Hewlett-Packard providing the silicon fabrication. When the student projects worked as planned, word of the simplified new methods spread throughout both the academic and business worlds and sparked an explosion in modern chip design, with the epicenter in Silicon Valley.

Conway's career trajectory skyrocketed, and her work gained numerous accolades. She was elected to the National Academy of

Engineering for her VLSI work. Conway also led the planning of the Department of Defense's Strategic Computing Initiative, a program that developed advanced computing and intelligent-weapons technology during the 1980s. She then moved on to serve as associate dean of engineering and professor of electrical engineering and computer science at the University of Michigan, in Ann Arbor.

Despite her professional successes, Lynn remained in "stealth mode" until 1999, fearful of the public scrutiny, the prejudice, and the violence her transsexuality might stir up. Then a researcher posted a message to a computing bulletin board looking for more information about IBM's secret "Project Y." This was the project that had paved the way for supercomputing, but all of the researcher's leads had run dry. After years of silence, Conway disclosed her knowledge of the project and revealed her involvement and the source of her silence. This self-outing led to reconciliation with her daughters and a reclaiming of her past, allowing her to publicly take credit for her groundbreaking work at IBM.

Lynn's work has transformed the world of computing. Look to her future contributions to facilitate a greater understanding of gender differences and melt away fear and prejudice about transsexuality. Expect nothing less from this brilliant mind.

And Let's Not Forget . . .

Carol A. Latham, president of Thermagon, created a breakthrough polymer that is used in "printed" computer circuit boards. The material's special heat-dissipating property is highly prized by computer notebook manufacturers and has been endorsed by industry heavy hitter Intel. . . . **Brenda Laurel** cofounded Purple Moon, a successful software company for girls, despite the conventional wisdom that says young women don't like computers. Laurel's research determined that the problem isn't that girls don't like computers—they just think that the boy-oriented, action-filled games on the market are boring. Purple Moon's games feature the things that most girls tend to prefer: character, story, and social complexity. . . . While volunteering at a hospital in 1985, **Leslie Dolman** encountered a disabled man who could neither speak nor write. Using her engineering background, she created a device that allowed him to work at a computer, and then she founded a nonprofit organization to distribute it and other computer-related aids for the disabled. . . . **Jan Davidson,** a high school teacher with an after-school tutoring business in Rancho Palos Verdes, California, invented "Math Blaster" software in 1982 and went on to author other bestselling titles. She later sold her company, Davidson & Associates, for more than $1 billion (yes, we said *billion*) and created a foundation that she now oversees. . . . **Zoriana Hyworon,** an entre-preneur from Manitoba, Canada, patented computer software that uses animation, graphics, and humor to create customized health and lifestyle assessments for improved personal well-being. Wellness Checkpoint is one of many programs she has developed over the last twenty-five years. . . . **Red Burns** was the first woman to establish a degree program for multimedia when she founded the Interactive Telecommunications Program at New York University in 1979. . . . **Sandra Kurtzig** of Atherton, California, was a twenty-five-year-old housewife and mother of two in 1985 when she began writing soft-ware to earn extra income. Ten years later this Silicon Valley pioneer had built ASK, a company with two hundred employees that earns $22 million in annual sales from its business-information systems. . . . Deaf students in classrooms with nondeaf students often find them-selves embarrassed by their inability to speak clearly enough to be understood. **Carrie Heeter** led a Michigan State research team that designed a computer program, the Personal Communicator, that gives the hearing-impaired the ability to type answers at a keyboard and let their laptop computer speak aloud to the class. . . . **Barbara Hayes-Roth** noticed that the free-flowing banter of online computer chat rooms can be intimidating to the neophyte. So she invented "virtual hosts" to show the Internet greenhorns the ropes. Dubbed Imps, her chat room guides greet people, encourage them to talk, and make introductions to others. Her characters include Erin, a slightly punk-ish bartender.

Genius in the Shadows:
The Women of ENIAC

The atomic bomb is historically thought to be the most significant technological development of World War II. After all, for better or worse, the top-secret Manhattan Project, which developed the nuclear device later detonated over Nagasaki and Hiroshima, Japan, in 1945, ushered in the Atomic Age and marked the beginning of the Cold War. Yet as the Cold War begins to fade into memory, it's the other major device developed by the U.S. Army during World War II that now seems destined to have the more important legacy—the computer. And the first people to operate the first computer and write its software program were a group of women who have been ignored by history.

The Electronic Numerical Integrator and Computer was the first-ever electronic general-purpose computer—the mother of all computers. ENIAC weighed in at thirty tons and was the size of a boxcar. It contained seventeen thousand vacuum tubes, seventy thousand resistors, and six thousand switches. Little wonder it was soon nicknamed "The Beast." Worse, for the six women mathematicians who were chosen to tame the beast, there was no computer software and no computer manual. They invented both.

At the time they were selected, Jean Jennings, Betty Snyder, Kathleen McNulty, Marlyn Wescoff, Frances Bilas, and Ruth Lichterman were part of a group of eighty women who had been hired by the army as "trajectory analysts." Their mission was pinpointing exactly where a bullet or artillery shell would be in the air every tenth of a second of its journey. To accomplish it entailed doing multiplication, square roots, long division, subtraction—a firing table for one gun might involve eighteen hundred trajectories, and the calculation of a single trajectory could take one woman a week to complete.

These women were essentially "human computers," who with adding machine, paper, and pencil calculated the incredibly complex firing tables that the army needed to vanquish the enemy on the battlefield. Working out of a row house on the campus of the University of Pennsylvania, they were a motley crew. Some were as young as eighteen, others as old as seventy. Some had formal mathematical training, some just a knack for numbers. The army observed that the women who excelled at the job tended to be patient, of course, and—less obviously—musically inclined.

The team of six who were selected to run ENIAC were at first asked to operate the computer with only paper diagrams of the machine to guide them. Classified by the army as "subprofessional," they didn't have the security clearance needed to be in the same room with ENIAC. After being handed the computer's entire stack of blueprints, the only instructions they received were these: "Figure out how it works, then figure out how to use it."

Even though all the women realized that the moment they got ENIAC up on its feet they were out of a job, they dove in and soon began referring to what they were doing as "programming." No operating systems, manuals, or computer languages existed. They were flying by the seat of their pants—or skirts, as it were.

By late 1945, after the war for which ENIAC was created had ended, security clearances were reluctantly granted and the women started programming ENIAC in earnest. This involved not just the setting of dozens of dials but also plugging heavy black cables into the face of the machine. Since each problem required a separate configuration of the cables, the women spent much of each day dragging the cables this way and that.

To streamline their efforts, the women programmers broke down differential equations into pieces, then figured out how long it would take ENIAC to solve each piece. Knowing this was crucial, because the machine had been created to perform multiple tasks simultaneously. However, since it took ENIAC longer to do multiplication than it did to do addition, the women had to compensate for the machine's weakness by timing it so that the right data hit the right spot at the right time. Relentless trial and error was their only hope—and it paid off.

In February 1946 the press watched in awe as ENIAC calculated the trajectory of a 155-millimeter shell in less time than it would take the bullet to land. Suddenly the Information Age had arrived. The creators of the machine, John Mauchly and Presper Eckert, chose not to mention to the reporters the six women's role in the breakthrough. To add insult to injury, the women weren't even invited to the celebratory dinner.

When the official picture of ENIAC was taken, it showed three women working on the computer, setting switches and inserting plugs. A man stands watching them. His expression is pompous and condescending. This picture repulsed the programmers so thoroughly that four of them quit the project. But the potential of computing was so exciting that Jean Jennings and Betty Snyder decided to stay on.

Jennings went to work with Adele Goldstine, a mathematician, as they turned ENIAC into a "stored-program" computer, eliminating the need for constant reconfiguration of the machine. Though John von Neumann is traditionally given credit for creating internal programming, it was actually Jennings who wrote the first code. While doing this, she did consult with von Neumann twice a month, but she thought he seemed more interested in flirting than mentoring.

In 1948 Jennings and Snyder went to work at Eckert-Mauchly and became involved in the creation of the Universal Automatic Computer—UNIVAC, the first general-purpose commercial computer. To make UNIVAC user friendly, Snyder created the C-10 instruction code, which allowed the device to be programmed by typewritten commands rather than dials and switches. The language she created was easy to remember: A stood for "add," B stood for "bring," etc.

Snyder also decided that the machine should be gray, and she inserted a numeric keypad to the right of the keyboard. These choices influenced the look of computers for decades.

She also led the development of a program that could organize payroll, track inventory, and manage data, making her the first person in history to use a computer to program its own application.

One thing Snyder realized during these years was that machines needed to talk the same language if computing were to spread. This knowledge impelled her to serve on the committee—headed by another woman, Grace Murray Hopper, profiled earlier in this chapter—that created COBOL: Common Business Oriented Language, a computer language still used around the world. Snyder was also instrumental in the development of the computer language FORTRAN.

However, in spite of all their accomplishments, Snyder and Jennings are not even mentioned in the MIT Press "definitive history" of computing. The book, by the way, is entitled A *Few Good* Men *from UNIVAC*. (Emphasis is ours.)

Lt. Col. Herman Goldstine, Adele Goldstine's husband, also wrote a book about the early days of computers. Despite the fact that he was there at the scene and watched the six women's contributions to history day after exasperating day, his book mentioned only their names and whom they came to marry. As word slowly seeped out that these ladies deserved massive credit for launching the boat of high technology, a reporter contacted Goldstine and asked him for an explanation of the gross oversight. He shrugged. "I was just trying to get the book done."

To this day, if you go to a library and check the index of a computer history book, you will not find the names of Jean Jennings, Betty Snyder, Kathleen McNulty, Marlyn Wescoff, Frances Bilas, and Ruth Lichterman. As far as posterity is concerned, they never existed. Perhaps most amazingly, the army failed to invite the women to the gala dinner commemorating the fiftieth anniversary of ENIAC. It wasn't until documentarian Kathryn Kleiman, who made a film about these pioneers, intervened that the army changed its mind.

CHAPTER 4

Medicine

I n the past decade more than half of the patents granted to women have been in chemistry. And the bulk of those mine the rich field of organic chemistry: new drugs, gene therapies, the stuff the future is made of. Maybe it's because the future is too new to have an old boys' network.

But of course women have always been healers. Long before Dr. Gerty Cori became the first woman to win the Nobel Prize for medicine in 1947. Before Elizabeth Blackwell became the first American woman to graduate medical school in 1849. Before Lady Mary Montagu introduced smallpox variolation in 1717 and reduced smallpox mortality in England from 30 percent to 2 percent. Before Lady Ana de Osorio introduced quinine to Europe in 1638 and cured malaria in Spain. Before Abbess Hildegard of Bingen, Germany, described blood circulation in the eleventh century. Before Julius was delivered by cesarean section—women were midwife and surgeon, herbalist and homeopath.

It has not always been safe for a woman to practice the healing arts. In Athens a woman studied or practiced "medicine or physic on pain of death." And while today we may think of burning witches at the stake as the stuff of drama, it was all too real. The Holy Office of the Inquisition proudly declared in 1554 that to date they had burned thirty thousand women alive. Some estimates put the total number of women killed for "witchcraft" between the fourteenth and seventeenth centuries as high as 3 to 9 million, a virtual holocaust. Their sin? They were midwives and herbalists.

In the twentieth century, Lydia Pinkham, for one, kept the art of herbal healing alive with her popular "patent medicine." Technically it was never patented, although Lydia Pinkham's Vegetable Compound was a registered trademark. Modern medicine scoffed at her botanical formula, saying that its alcohol content was its main palliative. But holistic neomodernists claim that its gentian/dogwood/pleurisy root/ black cohosh recipe is actually powerful naturopathy. In any event, it was a success; the Pinkham family business earned $3 million a year in the 1920s.

At the same time Louise Pearce was working in the Belgian Congo, devising a serum to cure sleeping sickness. In the 1930s Hattie Alexander developed an antibody for meningitis, reducing the death rate from that disease by 80 percent. In the 1940s Gladys Hobby refined penicillin and the antibiotic Terramycin, and Helen Taussig

It took forty-five patents, ten honorary doctorates, and a Nobel Prize for Dr. Gertrude Elion to finally enter the Inventors Hall of Fame. (Courtesy of the National Inventors Hall of Fame)

pioneered the blue-baby operation. In the 1950s Virginia Apgar saved untold newborn lives by devising the Apgar Score.

When Elizabeth Blackwell applied to Geneva Medical College, the all-male student body voted to admit her only as a joke. Times have changed. In 1868 Blackwell started the first medical school for women. In 1897 Johns Hopkins University officially opened its doors to women—because a wealthy benefactress made that a condition of her bequest.

The first woman to benefit from that injunction was Florence Sabin. She went on to divine the workings of the lymphatic system and of red corpuscles.

Gertrude Elion

CHEMOTHERAPY

The Inventors Hall of Fame was established in 1973 in Akron, Ohio. But it was almost twenty years before the organization finally inducted a woman, Dr. Gertrude Elion. This is what she had to do to be honored:

Discover the cure for childhood leukemia. Discover the first immunosuppressant, making kidney transplants possible. Develop treatments for gout and for herpes. Lay the groundwork for the development of AZT, the first drug to fight AIDS. Dr. Elion has forty-five patents to her name and twenty-five honorary doctorates. In 1988 she was awarded the Nobel Prize for Medicine. And yes, in 1991 the Inventors Hall of Fame finally inducted her.

Inducted her? Heck, they should have built a statue of her. If anyone typifies inventing genius, it is Dr. Gertrude Elion.

Calling the young Gertrude "precocious" is like calling Adolf Hitler "maladjusted"; it's true, but it doesn't go nearly far enough. This is a girl who in New York City in the 1930s started high school at the age of twelve and college at the age of fifteen. The daughter of a dentist, young Trudy chose to study chemistry because her beloved grandfather died of cancer in front of her, and she vowed to fight the disease that took him.

"It was a long, painful illness," remembered Elion. "After watching him die, I knew what I had to do."

Upon graduating summa cum laude in 1937 at the age of nineteen, Elion encountered two big obstacles to her mission: the Great Depression and the Great Boys' Club. They told her there was no point in hiring her, because she'd only get married and leave. One interviewer told her flat out that he wouldn't hire her because she was pretty; she would distract the men from their work.

So she went to secretarial school, and she did some nursing, and she waited. Eventually a chemist she met at a party said she could work in his lab, provided she didn't expect to get paid. She jumped at the chance.

Elion's enthusiasm and talent for lab work paid off: soon she was earning twenty dollars a week and all the coffee she could drink. She somehow used this to finance graduate courses at New York University, and earned a master's degree.

The most challenging job she could land, though, was as a chemistry teacher.

And then the Japanese bombed Pearl Harbor, and everything changed. Male chemist after male chemist marched off to war, and the Rosie the Riveters of the nation were joined by the Gertrude Elions.

After a stint and Johnson & Johnson, Elion went to pharmaceutical newcomers Burroughs-Wellcome, where she hoped to enter the world of drug research. Dr. George Hitchings was immediately taken with her understanding of the nucleic acid building blocks he worked with (Elion later admitted she really didn't understand half of what he was saying!) and offered her fifty dollars a week to start. The team stayed together for forty years.

Loyal to her teenage oath, Elion always focused her work on anti-cancer drugs. Her initial breakthrough was Purinethol, the first drug to treat leukemia. In 1957 she synthesized Imuram, which blocks rejection of foreign tissue and enabled the advent of earthshaking therapies like kidney transplants. Then her team came up with Zyloprim, for the treatment of gout, and later the important antiviral agent acyclovir (Zovirax), used to treat herpes.

She was once asked how many lives she had saved through her work. "Hundreds of thousands, anyway," she shyly admitted. "When you meet someone who has lived for twenty-five years with a kidney graft, there's your reward."

In 1967 Elion was named head of the Department of Experimental

Therapy at Burroughs-Wellcome. In 1983 she officially retired, although she continued to work for the World Health Organization and lecture worldwide. Elion died in 1999 at the age of eighty-one, but even today there are scientists at what is now the pharmaceutical conglomerate Glaxo-Wellcome who can proudly say, "Trudy Elion hired me!" Apparently she wasn't such a distraction after all.

Janet Rideout
AZT

One of the women who can claim that Trudy Elion hired her is Dr. Janet Rideout. The young organic chemist had written to Burroughs-Wellcome shortly before earning her Ph.D. from the State University of New York at Buffalo, mostly, says Rideout, "because they weren't far from where my parents lived, and because I had heard of them."

It turned out to be a good hire. Dr. Rideout went on to develop the first effective AIDS drug, AZT, a breakthrough treatment that not only extended and saved untold numbers of lives but earned Burroughs-Wellcome an estimated \$450 million per year. And even though AZT has been overshadowed in the news by the protease inhibitors invented by Katharine Holloway's and Chen Zhao's teams, AZT is still part of that "drug cocktail" that is finally making headway against HIV.

"When we first had the compound, we thought its life as a drug would only be a couple of years," marvels Rideout. "We expected other people to come up with different and better drugs sooner."

She sighs. "It's a devilish disease."

It was Rideout who first suggested testing AZT on the human immunodeficiency virus. Although it was a washout cancer drug abandoned twenty years earlier, Rideout saw potential in AZT. Using a revolutionary testing approach devised by her mentor, Dr. Elion, Rideout determined that AZT fought the retrovirus by tricking it into integrating with an inactive component in its DNA. It was the chemical equivalent of releasing sterile Medflies to combat an insect attack.

It took a lot of convincing, but in 1984 the National Institutes of Health blind-tested AZT along with fifty other wannabe drugs. Only

AZT worked. The FDA cut its red tape with a chain saw to rush approval of the drug; AZT was approved for patient use in 1987. On February 9, 1988, the Patent and Trademark Office granted Patent #4,724,232 to Janet Rideout and four other scientists who worked with her.

No, Dr. Rideout and her team didn't earn a big bonus, and they certainly don't get a share of the profits. Department head David Barry took the lion's share of the credit, and Rideout even had to go to court twice to protect her patents (she has forty in all, most related to AZT). But she wouldn't change a thing.

"We did what we enjoyed and were good at," she says. "I always thought it would be nice to do something good, instead of just commercial."

None of this would have happened had the young Janet gone on to teach high school, as was expected of her. A small-town girl from Vermont, a product of the public school system, she studied chemistry at Mount Holyoke College and, after earning a master's degree, was debating about going on for a teaching credential.

"At that point I found out you could earn your way through graduate school in the sciences by being an assistant," she recalls. She became the second full-time female student in her university's doctoral program.

She's since become a member of the board of directors of the American Institute of Chemists. She's been awarded the Distinguished Chemist Award from the North Carolina Institute of Chemists and is a member of the New York Academy of Sciences. And when she attends meetings, she's no longer the only woman in the room.

In 1998 Dr. Rideout was named vice president of cutting-edge research firm Inspire Pharmaceuticals, where she supervises the entire biology and chemistry departments. "It's a small biotech company," she says, "but we've established a good stable in the short time we've been in existence." In human terms that means that Dr. Rideout can go home and tell her chemist husband about the new drugs she's patenting, about how they ease the effects of chronic bronchitis and may even extend the life span of youngsters with cystic fibrosis.

"Maybe it sounds altruistic," says Rideout, "but I like having a positive effect on people's lives."

M. Katharine Holloway, Chen Zhao
PROTEASE INHIBITORS

Between 1994 and 1997 the mortality rate from AIDS in the United States plummeted by an astonishing 75 percent. The reason for that: protease inhibitors, drugs that block an enzyme vital to the replication of the HIV virus. In 80 percent of the patients taking the "drug cocktail" that features protease inhibitors along with AZT, the HIV virus can be reduced to below detectable levels.

Sharing the 1997 Inventor of the Year Award for developing these drugs were a team from Abbott Laboratories and a team from Merck Pharmaceuticals. The senior chemist from the Abbott team was a Beijing University graduate named Chen Zhao. And the molecular modeler on the Merck team was a an organic chemist from the University of Texas, M. Katharine Holloway.

Kate Holloway—born in Tupelo, Mississippi, to a telephone lineman and a stay-at-home mom, fifth of six children—was the first woman hired at Merck's computational group back in 1985. Five years later she did exactly what companies were always afraid would happen if they hired women: she got married and started a family.

"In fact, I was on maternity leave when the actual compound [Crixivan] was produced," she says, laughing. "But I had done the preliminary work, proved in a virtual sense that yes, this would work. So my name is on the patent."

Holloway came back to Merck after having her first baby in 1992; she came back after baby number two, as well. And when the company realized that motherhood isn't the end of the world—or even of a scientist's career—things changed.

"Today seven out of the twenty or so people in the department are women," says Holloway. "It's kind of amusing, because five of them were on maternity leave this year."

As a molecular modeler, Holloway uses computers to do hypothetically in an afternoon what it took an X-ray crystallographer like Rosalind Franklin months or even years to do. In the development of the protease inhibitor Crixivan, the challenge was to find a substance that could block the enzyme and not be metabolized by the patient.

"In drug development the tricky thing is to have it be potent against your target and also get to your target. It can be very potent in vitro, but if it doesn't work in vivo, it's worthless. And if it's soluble and not potent, that won't help, either."

Currently Holloway is once more on maternity leave; she and her chemist husband just welcomed baby number three. When she goes back, she will again be a "Jill of all trades" at Merck, working on bloodclotting agents, osteoporosis drugs, antihypertensives—"whatever program needs support." The area that excites her most is cardiovascular disease.

"Most people want to cure cancer," she says, "but that's not really my fantasy. My father died of a heart attack when he was forty-six, so that strikes much closer to home."

Unlike Holloway, Chen Zhao grew up surrounded by chemistry; both her parents are scientists. So is her husband; the two of them emigrated to the United States after earning their Ph.D.s at Beijing University, and both did postdoctoral work at Boston College.

"There are good opportunities in China, and no barriers to women," says Zhao. "But research conditions are much better here."

Zhao's husband, Qun Li, was the first to get a job offer at Abbott.

"He was called for an appointment on January fourth, 1990," recalls Chen Zhao. She remembers the date quite specifically, because "it was the due date of our first son. He said the lady from personnel assured him, 'No one ever has their baby on the due date.'"

Surprise, surprise. The elder Li brother's birthday is indeed January 4, 1990.

"My husband had to cancel his flight. We thought he would certainly lose the job, but they did agree to reschedule him." Not only did they hire Qun Li, but within two months they had hired his wife as well.

The youngest Ph.D. on her team, Zhao, like Holloway, was assigned to a protease inhibitor project and, like Holloway, sold her patent rights to her employer for one dollar. But she feels fairly recompensed for three years of teamwork, synthesizing thousands of different chemical compounds before finding Norvir.

"I think I'm pretty lucky," says Zhao. "If you can work on HIV, that's pretty interesting. And when people get better from our drug, you feel pretty happy."

Currently Zhao is working on drugs to cure that venerable scourge, influenza. Her bench-chemist approach balances and complements the virtual spin of the industry's Kate Holloways.

"Molecular modeling is getting better and better, but it isn't foolproof yet." Zhao smiles. "You still have to test the compound to see if it works!"

Elizabeth Hazen and Rachel Brown
NYSTATIN

The second and third women in the Inventors Hall of Fame were both inducted in 1994. That's because Elizabeth Lee Hazen and Rachel Fuller Brown worked as a team to develop nystatin, discovered in 1948 and introduced in 1954 as the world's first antifungal medicine. Nystatin cured everything from ringworm to athlete's foot to Dutch elm disease—it can even be used to restore paintings and books threatened by mildew. Nystatin earned $13 million for its inventors— and a whole lot more for its manufacturer, Squibb.

Penicillin, discovered in 1928 and introduced in 1941, was the first antibiotic proven safe and effective in the treatment of disease-producing bacteria. Nystatin was the first antibiotic proven safe and effective in the treatment of disease-producing fungi. (Even today, fungal diseases kill more people worldwide than do meningitis, syphilis, and rheumatic fever combined.) Between the two, doctors finally had tools that actually worked.

Nystatin got its name because microbiologist Hazen and chemist Brown were both working for the New York State Department of Health when they made their discovery: NY State. Nystatin. It took them six years to patent their fungicide, because the Patent Office wanted to see human trials first prove the "utility" of the drug.

But then nothing ever came easily to either woman.

Elizabeth Hazen was born dirt poor in rural Mississippi and orphaned at the age of three. Yet she managed to finance her own graduate studies in microbiology at Columbia University by working as a public school teacher.

Rachel Brown was from the more urban, if not urbane, Springfield, Massachusetts, but also poor: her father abandoned the family when

Elizabeth Hazen (left) and Rachel Brown earned but did not keep the $13 million from their invention of nystatin. (Courtesy of the National Inventors Hall of Fame)

she was twelve. It was thanks to a wealthy patron, a friend of the family, that she got an education.

The pair met in 1948, and Hazen, fourteen years older, was already considered a leading authority in fungi. Brown, the chemist, went to work to isolate the antitoxin in Hazen's samples. Within a year the pair had isolated the antifungal agent.

After announcing their discovery in 1950, Hazen and Brown were wooed by every major pharmaceutical house in the country with lucrative offers to produce the fungicide. Instead the duo patented the drug through a nonprofit research corporation. The fund generated $13 million in research grants, playing a key role in mycology for thirty years. Both women refused the fortune made by their invention, though. They continued to work in public health laboratories, subsist on their civil servants' salaries, and live and work until a ripe old age.

(Elizabeth Hazen died in 1975, just shy of her ninetieth birthday; Rachel Brown died in 1980 at age eighty-two.)

"If you have enough," Brown once said simply, "why should you want more?"

The partners did, however, take the $5,000 prize associated with the Squibb Award in Chemotherapy. And this time they were the *first* recipients.

Rosalyn Yalow

RADIOIMMUNOASSAY

Radioimmunoassay. It's a mouthful, but essentially it's the basis of nuclear medicine: using radioactive isotopes to diagnose everything from cancer to thyroid disease, diabetes to sterility. RIA can identify such tiny amounts of matter it's even used for forensic pathology, detecting minute levels of poison in the body.

Biochemist/physicist Dr. Rosalyn Yalow developed the revolutionary technique in a converted janitor's closet at the Veterans Administration Hospital in the Bronx, New York. It won her the Nobel Prize for Medicine in 1977.

This is what Dr. Yalow said about women in science when she accepted the honor: "The world cannot afford the loss of the talents of half its people if we are to solve the many problems which beset us."

The world might easily have dismissed Rosalyn Sussman Yalow's talents without a second thought. She was, after all, the daughter of Eastern European Jewish immigrants; during the Depression her father sold paper and string and her mother took in sewing. Still, Rosalyn managed to graduate Hunter College at age nineteen with degrees in chemistry and physics. When she applied to Purdue University for graduate school in 1941, Yalow (then still Sussman) was told that since, as one admissions officer put it, "she is from New York, she is Jewish, she is a woman," the chance of her finding a job in physics was nonexistent. There was no point even in admitting her.

She eventually got into Columbia University—as a secretary. But by then the war had so depleted the number of male graduate students that she was finally able to enroll at an unwelcoming University of

Illinois. She was the department's first female graduate student since World War I. It was there she met and married physicist Aaron Yalow.

The field of nuclear medicine exploded right after the first A-bombs did. By 1950 Yalow had joined forces with Dr. Solomon Berson and—while managing to raise two children and even keep a kosher home, no mean feat on its own—introduced radioimmunoassay in 1959. Had they patented the process, it would have made them rich; RIA is a $30 million-a-year business. But the duo chose to publish instead.

Dr. Berson died before he could accept the Nobel (it is never awarded posthumously), so Yalow alone accepted their share of the prize (physiologists Andrew V. Schally and Roger Guillemin were also honored that year). She was the second woman ever to win the Nobel for medicine, after Dr. Gerty Cori. In 1976 Yalow became the first woman to win the Lasker Basic Medical Research Award, and in 1988 she was given the National Medal of Science. Just imagine if the world had chosen to ignore her.

Helen Murray Free
URINALYSIS

Helen Murray Free became the fifth woman inducted into the Inventors Hall of Fame in 2000. Along with her husband, Alfred, she pioneered dry reagent urinalysis, making possible the "dip and read" home diabetes tests that save so many lives so simply.

Born Helen Mae Murray in Pittsburgh in 1923, she majored in chemistry at the College of Wooster in Ohio, graduating in 1944, and got a research job at Miles Laboratories—the Alka-Seltzer people. It was the beginning of a fifty-year career in the sciences. She married Albert Free in 1947, and, as a team, they revolutionized home health testing. Their books are the standards in the field.

Helen Murray Free holds seven patents for her work and has spent twenty years teaching others as a professor at Indiana University. Aside from the Inventors Hall of Fame, her honors include the Garvan Medal and an award given in her name by the American Chemical Society: the Helen M. Free Public Outreach Award.

Suzanne Ildstad

BONE MARROW TRANSPLANTS

On December 14, 1995, Dr. Suzanne Ildstad made the front page of newspapers nationwide when she presided over the first baboon bone marrow transplant in history. A San Francisco AIDS activist named Jeff Getty got special dispensation from the Food and Drug Administration to proceed with the highly experimental procedure, an eleventh-hour attempt to save him from the HIV virus that had ravaged his body since 1987.

It was Dr. Ildstad's discovery of the "facilitator cell" that made the thirty-minute operation possible. With facilitator cell technology, bone marrow can be transplanted from a nonmatching donor: a brother, a parent, even a neighbor—or a baboon. And baboons don't get AIDS.

"I never thought it would receive such a level of interest from the public and the press," says Ildstad. "It was overwhelming."

Technically the experiment was a failure: the xenotransplant survived for only two weeks. Yet the patient lived; as of this writing Jeff Getty thrives, against all odds.

In fact, he still corresponds with Dr. Ildstad's teenage daughter, Suzy. And Ildstad herself continues her work, using bone marrow transplants to effect cures for everything from diabetes to sickle cell anemia. "If people behave the way mice do," says Ildstad after a recent round of experiments at her Institute for Cellular Therapeutics in Louisville, Kentucky, "within the next five years autoimmune diseases can be cured."

A native of Edina, Minnesota, Suzanne Ildstad knew she wanted to be a doctor when she was five years old. Her mother and grandmother, after all, were nurses. Her grandmother, in fact, was scrub nurse to the famed Drs. Mayo. "In different times my grandmother would have been a doctor," Ildstad believes. "She was so proud when I graduated from medical school."

It's no coincidence that Ildstad graduated from the Mayo Medical School in 1978.

"It was still a pretty unusual career choice for a woman at that point," she says, "but my mom encouraged me to be a doctor instead of a nurse."

It was during the summer between the University of Minnesota and medical school that Ildstad met and married Stanford University graduate David Tollerud. Although trained as a mechanical engineer, Tollerud also had an interest in medicine; in fact, while still a student he had invented an apnea monitor to detect when sleeping babies stopped breathing. Today she oversees a staff of sixty at the Institute for Cellular Therapeutics, while he works nearby at the Allegheny Center for Environmental and Occupational Health.

They also go jogging with their son and daughter, grow their own herbs, cook pasta, and collect Victoriana. So much for anyone's preconceived notions of a couple of egghead research scientists.

Dr. Ildstad began her career as a pediatric surgeon, which she found wildly satisfying. "They have their whole lives ahead of them if the operation is a success," she says of her tiny patients. "I'll open the mail now and find a letter with the picture of a healthy, happy eight-year-old grinning at me."

Doing cutting-edge surgeries like organ transplants and bone marrow grafts, Ildstad was faced with the same dilemma as everyone else in the field: rejection. Not rejection by her patients but rejection by the patients' bodies. Either the host body will reject the transplanted organ (host versus graft disease), or else healthy bone marrow will fight off the body it has been transplanted into (graft versus host disease).

Ildstad's 1992 discovery of the facilitator cell (the lightbulb went off for her while she was jogging) and her purification of experimental amounts in 1993 changed everything.

Soon patients should be able to tolerate organ transplants without years of the immune-suppressing drugs invented by Dr. Gertrude Elion. They will be able to tolerate transplants from unrelated donors. They may even be able to tolerate transplants from unrelated species.

"To put it in perspective," says Dr. Ildstad, "the number of organ donors has not increased in the United States since 1988. In this country alone, at least thirty thousand people die per year waiting for a potentially lifesaving transplant.

"So either we top out at four thousand liver transplants a year and three thousand or so heart transplants, or we find an alternative solution."

Dr. Ildstad's solutions are working. Her latest experiments grafted "chimeric" (mixed, nonmatching) bone marrow into thirty-nine leukemia patients. She hoped for a 30 percent success rate, and to date all thirty-nine patients have accepted the transplants.

Ida Rolf
ROLFING

Today your company health insurance policy likely covers chiropractic care. It probably covers acupuncture, homeopathy, and massage therapy, too. But back in the 1920s and 1930s, when Dr. Ida Rolf pioneered "body work" as a healing technique, people pretty much thought she was crazy.

Rolf earned a Ph.D. in biochemistry from Columbia University in New York in 1916. She was always interested in alternative thinking, however, and studied yoga along with physiology. Her theory—she called it a discovery—was that the network of connective tissue encasing our muscles gets pulled out of alignment through time, use, and gravity. And by realigning the connective tissue, or fascia, we can realign the muscles and organs of the body. This realignment relieves symptoms of everything from asthma to migraine, backache to carpal tunnel syndrome.

Rolf was working as a researcher at the Rockefeller Institute when she perfected her method of body manipulation. It was an exciting time for alternative healing, a time when Fritz Perls was pioneering Gestalt therapy and John Bennett popularized the Gurdjieff School. Much of Rolf's experimentation was done at the famed counterculture center, the Esalen Institute at Big Sur in California.

Ida Rolf was already seventy-five years old when she founded the Rolf Institute. (Courtesy of the Rolf Institute)

It's easy to giggle at the touchy-feely therapies of the sixties. Thing is, the seventies, eighties, and nineties, and so on have proven that they work. Rolfing alone has been credited with saving Starkey Laboratories, one of Minnesota's largest manufacturers, more than $1 million a year in workers' compensation costs.

Ida Rolf founded the Rolf Institute in Boulder, Colorado, in 1971. She was seventy-five years old and still active. Today there are Rolf Institutes in Germany, Australia, and Brazil. All Rolfers—and there are only about nine hundred in the world—have to be certified by the Rolf Institute.

Ida Rolf died in 1979. The institute in Colorado celebrates her birthday each year by offering free Rolfing to children under the age of sixteen, a tradition Rolf herself began the day she turned eighty.

Patricia Bath
LASER CATARACT SURGERGY

In the movie *Tommy* it's Tina Turner who magically "gives eyesight to the blind." In real life the honor goes to Dr. Patricia Bath. We doubt that Dr. Bath would be offended if we point out that the two women rather look alike, as well.

The first African-American woman to receive a patent for a medical invention, Dr. Bath in fact has four patents for the advanced fiber-optic tool called the laserphaco. Essentially the laserphaco is a tiny probe through which laser pulses are transmitted directly into a cataract. The cataract is emulsified, as it were, and extracted from the eye—neatly, quickly, safely, and relatively inexpensively. And since 95 percent of us will develop cataracts if we live long enough, this is good news indeed.

Born in Harlem in 1942, "Patsy" Bath was raised in a loving but decidedly unscientific home. Her father was a merchant seaman from Trinidad; her mother was a cleaning lady. It was the blind woman on the corner who sold shopping bags, says Bath, who inspired her to work in ophthalmology.

As a seventeen-year-old science prodigy, Bath was awarded a fellowship to Yeshiva University and later a scholarship to Hunter

Neither racism nor sexism deterred Dr. Patricia Bath from her goal of preventing cataract blindness. (Courtesy of Patricia Bath)

College. When Hunter asked her for an estimate of her living expenses to calculate their grant, Bath says her parents replied, "Tell them you're fine. You don't need anything."

"Of course there were things I certainly could have used, like clothes," she remembers laughingly today. "But their attitude was 'the Lord will provide.'"

Bath aced her classes at Hunter and went on to Howard University Medical School, specializing in oncology. She switched to ophthalmology in her third year there because, she says, it was a field where you could see immediate, concrete results.

"The ability to restore vision," she says, "is the ultimate reward."

Bath went on to the Drew-King Medical Center in Los Angeles, where she cofounded the ophthalmology training program. In 1975 she became the first woman ophthalmologist on the UCLA faculty—although, she recalls, her reception there was somewhat chilly. "They offered me a basement office, away from the regular staff," she says. "I demanded equal treatment and the best of what they had to offer." She got it. In 1983 she became the first woman chair of the ophthalmology department.

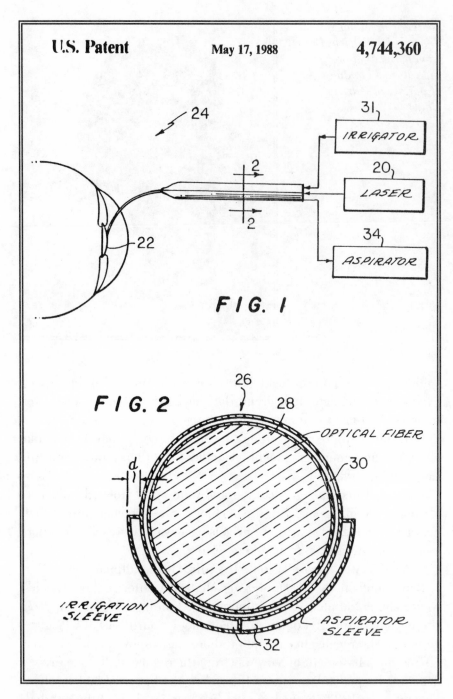

FIG. I

FIG. 2

The Laserphaco is only one of four patents for ophthalmic devices held by Dr. Patricia Bath.

Dr. Bath began work with YAG and excimer lasers in the 1980s, moving to France to do much of her research so as not to be hindered by slow, constricting FDA red tape. After years of laborious experimentation and a certain amount of resistance due to sexism and racism, the first of Bath's four patents was awarded in 1988.

She then took her technology to Nigeria, Pakistan, and war-torn Yugoslavia, where the blind were too poor even to hope for a cure. It would be impossible at this point to estimate the number of individuals whose eyesight has been restored by Dr. Bath's innovations.

Today Bath remains one of a handful of surgeons nationwide who can perform keratoprosthesis surgery: insertion of an artificial cornea to restore sight to people blinded by scar tissue. In the late 1990s she moved from Los Angeles to Howard University Hospital in Washington, D.C.—partly to be near her daughter, Eraka, who is enrolled there. In the medical school, of course.

Dr. Bath is looking forward to the day that, if not she, then at least her daughter can be referred to not as "a great black surgeon" but simply as "a great surgeon."

"And," she says, twinkling, "maybe Spike Lee will be called 'a great director' instead of 'a great black director,' too."

Diane Pennica

T-PA

Activase, the commercial name for tissue plasminogen activator or t-PA, has earned more than $1 billion for the drug company Genentech. More important, it saves the lives of 80 percent of heart attack victims who get it in time, it is used in combination with angioplasty to prevent heart attacks from happening in the first place, and it is proving effective in the treatment of strokes. It is one of the major drug advances of the last decade, and one of three names on the patent is Diane Pennica.

Her success in cloning t-PA earned Dr. Pennica the Inventor of the Year Award from the Intellectual Property Owners in 1989. She has been nominated for induction into the National Inventors Hall of Fame and also nominated for the prestigious Lemelson-MIT Prize.

She has been honored by her alma mater, the State University of New York, by the *New York Times*, and by Vice President Al Gore. She holds five patents for genetically engineered medicines and has filed for two more.

And none of this would have happened if she hadn't been mistaken for a schoolgirl.

It was May 1980. Pennica, a carpenter's daughter from upstate New York, was a newly minted Ph.D. microbiologist just hired by an upstart start-up company called Genentech. And since she was the house expert on cloning thrombolytics—substances that dissolve blood clots—Genentech sent her to represent them at a cardiology conference in Malmö, Sweden.

Pennica was twenty-nine years old, five feet tall, and jet-lagged. When she got to the hotel, she was told that the meeting she thought was beginning the next day had already started. She raced into the conference room still wearing her hot pink travel sweatshirt. And she listened and took notes as Dr. Désiré Collen, the top researcher in the field, explained the significance of the rare blood protein t-PA, nature's own clot buster.

"It turned out," Pennica says years later, "that I had accidentally walked into an advance meeting of all the top people in the field. The only reason they didn't kick me out was that they thought I was one of the speakers' daughters, just waiting patiently for her dad.

"I was an intruder. They said if I had been a guy, they would have thrown me out. It was sheer luck and fate that I was at that meeting. If I had attended only the regular conference, I might not have met Désiré or recognized the importance of his research."

Pennica convinced Collen to let her clone t-PA, in order to produce sufficient quantities to make it commercially available. And then she worked fifteen hours a day for the next two years to make good her promise.

"That's how you beat the competition," says Pennica. "You work harder than anybody else."

Cloning the gene that encoded t-PA's twisted chain of 527 amino acids was no easy task. But in July 1982 Diane Pennica received a standing ovation at a medical conference in Switzerland when she announced her success.

Still, says Pennica, that ovation was nothing compared to the hug she got later that same year from a man named Steve Birnbaum—the first heart attack patient treated with Activase.

"One of the marketing people told Steve that I was the woman who cloned t-PA," she says. "He grabbed me and hugged me and said 'thank you, thank you—your drug saved my life.' That was the high point of my whole career."

Another high point for Pennica came in 1990, when she married attorney Frank E. Hagle. But there have been low points, too. In 1987 she lost her mother.

"My mother died from colon cancer," says Pennica. "So now I'm involved in cancer research. My mother's death gave me a lot of incentive to try and make a contribution in this area."

Andrea Bodnar

TELOMERASE

How would you like to be the person who cures cancer and discovers the secret of immortality? Andrea Bodnar just might turn out to be that person. Not a bad résumé for a thirty-five-year-old research biochemist from Toronto.

Dr. Bodnar was team leader at the Geron Corporation in Northern California, the team that cloned the enzyme telomerase and finally broke the "Hayflick Limit," allowing human cells to live twice their normal life span. The accomplishment made the front pages of newspapers around the world, turning the shy Bodnar into an overnight celebrity.

"One doesn't expect this when one becomes a scientist," she says smiling.

Inspired by genetics groundbreakers like Nobel Prize laureate Barbara McClintock, DNA mapper Rosalind Franklin, and enzymologists Maude Menton and Leonor Michaelis, Bodnar earned a Ph.D. in biochemistry from McMaster University in Hamilton, Canada—the only female graduate student in her department. Her summer jobs were in a lab, and "I couldn't imagine a more fun way to spend my life," she recalls. She was working as a cell biologist when she was invited to join Geron. And that's where she made history in January 1998.

Backstory: In 1961 cell biologist Leonard Hayflick showed that cells taken from a living person will divide only a limited number of times. This is why we age and die.

But what makes it so? In the 1970s DNA pioneers Francis Crick and James Watson theorized that every time a chromosome replicates itself, the very end of the chromosome—the telomere—keeps getting shorter. Picture the tip of a shoelace over time: with each cell renewal the telomere gets increasingly frayed. And so with every replication the cell becomes more and more distorted, like a much-copied videotape, until it withers and dies.

What controls the life span of the telomere—and hence the life span of the cell itself—is an enzyme called telomerase. Telomerase was discovered in 1992 and ever since then scientists had been racing to synthesize it. After all, synthetic telomerase could literally be immortality in a bottle.

In the summer of 1997 Dr. Andrea Bodnar's team finally cloned the protein that made telomerase. Then came the proof of the pudding: introducing it into human cells. Would they divide more often? Would they live longer? Could this magic bullet actually slow down or even reverse the aging process?

"That's when we were really biting our nails," remembers Bodnar. "The experiment started in the summer . . . and we watched the cells divide until December. They lived well beyond the Hayflick Limit."

The cells had lived twice as long as they should have, and they thrived. "Not only have they divided past the Hayflick Limit," says Bodnar, "but they look and act like young cells."

While the average consumer can't wait to mainline telomerase in hopes of living forever (and looking good the whole time), this is not Geron's objective. The immediate goal is to create drugs for age-related diseases, like Alzheimer's. Bodnar already holds a patent for one such compound.

The flip side of cells that die too soon, of course, is cells that live forever. Cancer cells are immortal, and yes, one of the changes that happens when cells go rogue is that they produce too much telomerase.

"If you can inhibit the telomerase production in cancer cells," explains Bodnar, "you should be able to induce cancer cells to go through the normal process of aging. This is the first step."

Immortality and the cure for cancer. Not a bad day's work. Of course, the day-to-day job itself is exacting, painstaking, and some would even say boring.

"I love what I do!" Bodnar glows when she says it. "I absolutely love it. It's the most exciting and challenging way to spend my days. Working in the lab . . . well, and sailing. And, you know, the sails are made of Kevlar, and I never knew that was invented by a woman."

Early Innovators

The earliest medical textbooks, *Practica Brevia* and *De Compositione Medicamentorum*, were copied by hand and passed down from doctor to doctor, generation after generation. Both these books—as well as *Passionibus Mulierum Curandorum* ("The Diseases of Women")—were written by the same remarkable eleventh-century physician. Many histories credit the works to a man named Trottus. In fact, all were written by a woman named **Trotula** (died 1097).

Daughter of a noble family and married to fellow physician John Plataerius, Trotula lived and worked in Salerno, Italy. She was the first physician on record to promote cleanliness, exercise, a balanced diet, and stress avoidance for health maintenance. She developed surgical techniques and taught diagnostic methods that were used for centuries. Her herbal tinctures and salves not only were standard operating procedure for medieval healers but are being rediscovered even today.

Inventor, poet, mother of three, and ob/gyn to the queen, **Louyse Bourgeois** (1563–1638) was also the first person ever to prescribe iron as a treatment for anemia. She invented some of the earliest obstetrical instruments and delivered more than two thousand babies in her career—including King Louis XIII of France in 1601. Her book, *Observations*, was a landmark treatise in its day.

A South African plant used to treat syphilis and gonorrhea before the advent of sulfa drugs was discovered by a Dr. James Barry—whose name was really **Miranda Stuart** (1797–1865). Obviously a wildly intelligent young woman, Stuart graduated Edinburgh College of Medicine at the age of fifteen—in the guise of "a frail young man."

She entered military service and remained disguised as Dr. James Barry for her entire career. Dr. Barry's ruse was so successful that "he" was even named surgeon general of Canada. When an autopsy revealed the late Dr. Barry as the late Miss Stuart, a planned military funeral was promptly canceled.

Florence Nightingale (1820–1910) invented something you can't patent: the modern hospital. A child of privilege who cared more for sick animals than for afternoon teas, she became a nurse on the suggestion of two nuns she met in Egypt. In 1854 the Crimean War began, and Nightingale was appointed Britain's superintendent of nurses in Turkey.

When she arrived, she discovered that the hospital consisted of a four-mile-long row of beds—constructed on top of a cesspool. She changed everything: the water, the diet, the record keeping, the physical plant. Thanks to her ceaseless efforts, the mortality rate was reduced from 42 percent to 2 percent in less than a year.

In 1876 Nightingale sent a blueprint for a state-of-the-art hospital to Johns Hopkins University; they built it without changing a line. Hospitals look the way they look today because that's the way Florence Nightingale, "the Lady with the Lamp," designed them.

Medical researchers had debated for decades over the origin and function of the lymphatic system, until **Florence Sabin** (1871–1953) made the invisible visible by staining lymphatic fluid with ink. When she published her research paper in 1902, scientific common knowledge was turned on its head.

Sabin spent years studying the lymphatic and circulatory systems—she's credited with discovering how red corpuscles are made—but there's a bust of her in the National Statuary Hall in Washington, D.C. because of her work in public health. She represents the state of Colorado, and since each state is allotted only two statues and Colorado used one for a fiery, feisty feminist, it's obvious Sabin's work made quite an impact on her adopted hometown of Denver.

Jonas Salk might never have become a household name if it weren't for **Lilian Vaughan Morgan** (1870–1952). It was she who invented the first polio vaccine for primates. A zoologist who turned her attention to the new science of genetics at the start of the last century, Morgan confirmed Nettie Stevens's theory of X and Y chromosomes by identifying the X chromosome on fruit flies in 1921.

Morgan eventually published a total of sixteen scientific papers, and inspired her daughter, Isabel Morgan, also to fight the scourge of polio. In 1944 Isabel Morgan became the only woman on the Johns Hopkins poliovirus team.

And Let's Not Forget . . .

According to her family, one **Mrs. Shipley** of Annapolis, Maryland, developed the concept of "buffered" (acid-neutralized) aspirin while an employee at Bristol-Meyers. Bufferin became a staple product of the firm. . . . **Susan Skewes** retired from nursing a wealthy woman thanks to Patent #5,702,992—the Bag Bath. A sterile, pH-balanced system for bathing patients, the product has taken Skewes, as she puts it, "from bags to riches." . . . Mother and daughter **Lisa Vallino** (a nurse) and **Betty Rozier** (an entrepreneur) conceived, patented, and distribute the I.V. House, a sterile plastic dome that keeps small children from pulling intravenous catheters out of their arms. . . . Australian housewife **Joan Stuckey** calls her 1980 invention the Push Cush. A silly name for an important tool: the fluid-filled device helps bedridden patients tone muscles that would otherwise atrophy. The device has also been important to Stuckey herself—it's made her a millionaire. . . . **Janine Jagger,** M.P.H., Ph.D., has patented six safety-needle devices to keep doctors from contracting blood-borne diseases like AIDS and hepatitis. In 1988 the Intellectual Property Owners gave her its Distinguished Inventor Award. . . . Working unheralded behind the Iron Curtain in the 1970s and '80s, chemical engineer **Blagina Vassileva** has invented twenty-five different antibiotics, useful in treating humans, animals, and even plants. . . . **Maria Bade** holds Patent #4,958,011 for artificial skin. . . . **Lydia Aguilar Bryan** and her husband, Joseph Bryan, in 1996 isolated the protein that causes hyperinsulinism, a discovery that may lead to Aguilar's lifelong goal: a cure for diabetes. . . . In 2000, **Dr. Nancy Davis** and her partner, Dr. Robert E. Johnson, were on the cusp of developing an AIDS vaccine. . . . About 15 million new cases of sexually transmitted diseases are diagnosed each year in the United States. **Ann-Marie Corner** is president of Biosyn, a Philadelphia company that has developed a "microbicide," a chemical compound that can be used topically by women to kill a variety of viruses and bacteria. The gel, which will be marketed under the name Savvy, has shown in early clinical trials that it eliminates pathogens by attaching itself to their membranes. . . . In 1998 psychologists **Martha K. McClintock** and **Kathleen Stern** finally distilled the elusive human pheromone: an odorless chemical that influences people's sexual behavior. You know, the stuff they've been pretending to put in expensive perfume for years. . . . **Barbara S. Askins** was named Inventor of the Year in 1979 for her autoradiographic image-enhancement system, which provided a real peek at the inner workings of the cell. . . . **Jewell L. Osterholm** won Inventor of the Year in 1985 for a new way to treat strokes. . . . And the 1998 Inventor of the Year Award was shared by the seven Oncormed researchers who identified the gene that causes most breast cancers and devised a test to determine which women were susceptible to such cancers. The team comprised **Patricia D. Murphy, Antonette C. Allen, Brenda S. Criz, Sheri J. Olson, Denise Schelter Thurber, Bin Zeng,** and—the lone male—Christopher P. Alvarez.

CHAPTER 5

Mother Earth

C an there be any doubt that in the earliest civilizations the gatherers advanced agriculture through invention and innovation while the boys were out hunting? It was most likely a woman who first cultivated a crop, domesticated an animal, and fashioned a plow.

Mother Earth has always been a focus of distaff ingenuity. The first woman patent holder in America, colonist Sybilla Masters, received English Patent #401 in 1715 for a machine to process Indian corn. Thirty years later Georgia plantation owner Elizabeth Lucas Pinckney introduced America's first cash crop, indigo, loosening forever the British crown's grip on the colonies' economic dependence.

At the dawn of the nineteenth century a young widowed mother in France transformed the sparkling wine industry by inventing a method for clarifying champagne—the *remuage* system—which would be adopted by all other vintners and is still in use. The "La Veuve Clicquot" (literally "the widow Clicquot") label, which continues to grace bottles of some of the world's finest champagne, is testament to her imagination.

A generation later another Frenchwoman anticipated the need for a cheap, plentiful source of fertilizer. In 1859 a Parisian named Mme Lefebre patented the process for making nitrates out of nitrogen gas. Previously, nitrate fertilizer was available only through natural mineral deposits, which by the 1920s would be seriously depleted.

The advent of the Industrial Age brought a new type of environmental awareness. Modern times has no patent on air pollution; the problem is well over a hundred years old. (The "fog" that covered the trail of Jack the Ripper in late-nineteenth-century London was actually a thick smog produced by coal-burning factories.) Nor were American industrial cities immune to noxious fumes. In 1879 Mary Walton, a resident of Manhattan, received Patent #221,880 for a technique that deflected factory smoke into water tanks, where the pollutants were trapped and then transported into the sewage system.

There's no evidence Mary Walton's antismog system was ever used, but in 1891 the City of New York bought another of her patented devices—the first to reduce noise pollution. The city's newly installed elevated trains produced an intolerable clamor. Walton devised an apparatus for cradling the rails in a frame of cotton, tar, and sand. The problem had been tackled unsuccessfully by the country's most noted machinists and inventors, Thomas Edison among them.

Across the Atlantic, English entomologist Eleanor Omerod was, for the first time, applying scientific methods to pest control. Her commonsense remedies were widely published, and at the time of her death in 1901 no less than the *Times* of London declared that she had "revolutionized" agriculture.

One of the earliest ecologists was Ellen Swallow Richards, whose studies of water pollution date back to the 1870s. It was in the first half of the twentieth century that Ruth Patrick studied freshwater ecosystems as complex universes, setting the stage for the modern environmental movement. (Her work would later be expanded by Rachel Carson, author of the 1960 book *Silent Spring*, which called attention to the reckless uses of pesticides and herbicides.) Patrick established that the microscopic diatom, a single-celled alga, was the building block for an entire food chain. By measuring the number of diatoms—with a small device she invented called the diatometer—one could determine the "health" of a lake or river as well as the presence of pollutants that might otherwise go undetected.

Today, as the coming profiles will attest, women excel in both harnessing and protecting Mother Nature.

Sally Fox
FoxFibre

In 1982 Sally Fox was a young scientist with an unusual hobby: hand spinning. In 1992 she was named Entrepreneur of the Year thanks to an unlikely synergy between those two interests. The product of that synergy bears her name: FoxFibre.

It all started when a friend of Fox's father's gave her some cotton seeds to study for their pest-resistant qualities. (She was trained as an entomologist and never saw a cotton plant until she was age twenty-four.) Turned out those seeds didn't grow into your basic long-staple white cotton. They grew into brown cotton. Thanks to years of study and crossbreeding, that cotton now grows in every color from pale green to ebony.

What's the point of cotton that grows in colors? The advantages are numerous: first, the dyes that turn white cotton into pale green or ebony are extremely toxic. Second, they are extremely expensive. Not only is fabric made of FoxFibre more environmentally friendly than conventional dyed cotton, it's 30 percent cheaper. Also, naturally colored cottons are innately more fire resistant than white cotton, and, rather than fading, cloth made from colored cotton actually intensifies in hue with repeated washings.

Now, colored cotton is not a miraculous innovation. The original khaki fabric was made in India from naturally brown cotton bolls. But colored cotton grew only in short-staple bolls; the fibers weren't long enough for machine spinning. Fox's great advance—made possible by her understanding of spinning and weaving—was to grow long-staple colored cotton. Cotton that could be machine woven.

You'd think that textile manufacturers everywhere would jump at this new product, but at first Fox encountered only resistance. Then a FoxFibre sweater in the L. L. Bean catalog sold out in a record six days. And then a Japanese mill purchased half of Fox's crop. And then came the awards for her company, Natural Cotton Colours: the Edison Award for Most Innovative Company, the Green Housekeeping Award for Environmental Leadership, the Discover Award for Technological Innovation, even the Good Housekeeping Seal of Approval.

Yet Fox's road to success has seen its share of potholes. An innovation that should have been embraced by the cotton industry was, on second thought, viewed as a threat. L. L. Bean, then Levi's and Land's End dropped their FoxFibre product line in quick succession. Fox blames white-cotton growers, who closed ranks and pressured mills to stop handling her colored cotton. In 1996 her company was forced to declare bankruptcy as sales dwindled from a high of $10 million to $1.2 million.

Nevertheless, she's confident all this is a temporary setback. Natural Cotton Colours still retains an enviable roster of corporate clients, including IKEA, Jockey, and Fieldcrest-Cannon, and business is booming in Europe, where environmentally conscious customers are attracted to its organically grown cotton.

Today Sally Fox, at forty-five, oversees six hundred acres of experimental cotton fields in western Arizona. She sees to it that the manufacturers who work with FoxFibre are environmentally friendly and politically correct. She rides her horse and plays with her three Border collies and comes up with new ways to genetically engineer cotton through crossbreeding.

"I think there's something really different about these colors than the dyed version of these colors," says Fox confidently. "I think people sense it and feel it and they're very comfortable with it. As we become better known, the environmental benefits become better known, demand will increase."

Virginia Dale
ECO-SOFTWARE

If Virginia Dale was looking for a sign that she had chosen the right career, she got it big time the day she defended her doctoral dissertation. She was receiving her Ph.D. at the University of Washington, Seattle, in the little-known field of mathematical ecology ("using mathematical relationships to understand ecological interactions," she explains). It was March 21, 1980. And a hundred miles away Mount Saint Helens blew its top.

Dale was one of eight ecologists invited to the site to document reemerging plant life following the volcano's megablast. The chance to study an ecosystem being born again at ground zero was too tempting to pass up, even though Dale was a new mother with an eight-month-old daughter. Determined not to miss the first trek to the volcano, Dale brought along a breast pump to feed her still-nursing baby.

The end result of her studies was a computer program that predicts the consequences of land use. This tool has proved invaluable in allowing policy analysts to make intelligent choices—and in providing ecologists with fodder for protest when they don't.

"Instead of going out and applying a policy and then twenty years later seeing what the impact is," Dale says, "they can sit down to a computer and, like a game, see what the impact may be."

The work at Mount Saint Helens required meticulous and arduous record keeping, giving Dale the raw material she needed for her work.

"We have a fifteen-year baseline," said Dale in 1997. "It's the only long-term record of its kind." But is it possible to *virtually* duplicate that kind of data? The question led her to invent her eco-software. Today she brings her laptop computer into the field along with a pick and shovel.

Recently Dale used her invention in Brazil's Rondônia province, which has the dubious distinction of being the "deforestation capital of the world." Her software projected how much more profitable the land would be if simple tree cultivation and crop diversification were used. The Brazilian government is currently reviewing her land-use policy recommendations—recommendations often strongly opposed by agribusiness.

Dale recalls the time a colleague at Brazil's Department of the Environment presented her with a jacket emblazoned with the department's name. She donned the gift with effusive thanks and was surprised when everyone in the room laughed. Apparently department agents were so hated by the settlers in the region that many had received death threats. "The joke is that you're a target," she says.

Allene Rosalind Jeanes
Xanthan Gum, IV Fluids

Next time you pick up a bottle of steak sauce, salad dressing, cough medicine, or prescription liquid medication, check the label. Odds are the "magic" ingredient that holds everything together is a cereal starch called xanthan gum, or just xanthan. With sales of more than $50 million in the food industry alone, xanthan is one of the most widely used thickening and stabilizing agents in the world.

The research team that created this commercial wonder was led by Dr. Allene Rosalind Jeanes, a biochemist with the U.S. Department of Agriculture. And if that accomplishment weren't enough to crown thirty-five years of government service, she went on to develop IV fluids, which revolutionized emergency room care and saved countless lives.

In the 1950s the USDA's research arm was charged with the task of establishing new commercial applications for the nation's domestic cereal grains. At the time most thickening and stabilizing agents were imported—a costly venture. The Jeanes team applied its knowledge of microbiology and biochemistry and invented an entirely new type of gum, a water-soluble polysaccharide that had thickening *and* stabiliz-ing *and* suspending action.

Because the new gum was unaffected by heat, xanthan even found application in the oil and natural gas industries (mixing it with the drilling muds used in exploration gave the mud the proper consis-tency). By 1996, sales of xanthan topped $100 million annually.

Born in 1906 in Waco, Texas, Jeanes was the child of a working-class family. Her father was a switchman for the St. Louis Southwest-ern Railroad. By high school, her extraordinary intellect was already being recognized, and upon graduating with honors, she enrolled at Baylor University, majoring in chemistry. Again she graduated with "highest honors" and went on to earn a master's degree in organic chemistry at the University of California, Berkeley. After teaching col-lege science courses for five years, she returned to graduate school, where she earned a Ph.D.

Today a scientist with Jeanes's credentials would be courted by the leading drug companies, and in fact, it was her great desire to pursue her pharmaceutical research. But this was 1938, with the Great Depression still gripping the nation, and the male enclave of private-sector biochemistry was not about to hire a woman.

The pharmaceutical industry's loss was a gain for the USDA. She was hired in 1941 as an assistant chemist at the National Center for

Agricultural Utilization Research in Peoria, Illinois, just three months after the laboratory was opened. The focus of her research at first was the study of the basic structure of starch and, specifically, a component of starch called dextran.

In 1950 Jeanes wrote a paper proposing that dextran might be the key to the long-sought substitute for blood plasma. It was a startling theory, but the timing could not have been better. The United States had just entered the Korean War; a blood plasma substitute was needed to save lives. A crash program was started at the Peoria research unit involving eighty scientists, including microbiologists, biochemists, and bioengineers under the auspices of the Department of Defense. Jeanes and her immediate research group played the pivotal role.

Less than a year after the project began, a dextran-based agent that could be used to expand blood plasma volume was saving lives on the battlefield. While "clinical dextran"—more commonly known as IV fluids—cannot replace blood, the fluid will keep blood pressure up until the body can manufacture more blood.

In the process of creating IV fluids, Jeanes and her research team isolated dextran from more than a hundred bacterial strains. Not only did this research become the foundation for their discovery of xanthan, but it was also used by other scientists in immunology and immunochemistry.

Jeanes became the first woman to receive the USDA's Distinguished Service Award for her work on IV fluids. For formulating xanthan, she and her biopolymer research unit were honored with the USDA Superior Service Award. Among her many lifetime honors, Jeanes became a member of the National Academy of Sciences National Research Council, received the U.S. Civil Service Commission Woman's Award, was given the highest award from the American Chemical Society, and was accepted into the USDA's Hall of Fame. By the time of her death in 1995, she held ten patents and published over sixty scholarly articles.

During the Korean War a colleague of Jeanes's wrote about the importance of her invention of IV fluids. Witnessing the recovery of a wounded soldier, he wrote, "He might have died—not from the injury itself, but because he went into shock. Yet he lives—because of dextran."

Odette Shotwell
AGRICULTURAL ANTIBIOTICS

Mary Ollidene Weaver
SUPER SLURPER

Allene R. Jeanes was not the only woman researcher of note at the U.S. Department of Agriculture. There was also Ruth Benerito, credited elsewhere in this chapter for her invention of wash-and-wear cotton. And there were two women at the USDA's national research center who combined chemistry and biology to achieve noteworthy results:

- Odette Shotwell developed analytical tests for detecting toxic fungi on crops and subsequently patented four antibiotics; she is personally credited with keeping the carcinogen aflatoxin out of the food chain.

- Mary Ollidene Weaver was part of the research team that developed Super Slurper, a highly absorbent breakthrough polymer used in everything from oil filters to disposable diapers.

Why did all three scientists end up at the USDA research unit in Peoria, Illinois? Little is known about Weaver's personal life, but Shotwell's reason for working at the federal center was the same as Jeanes's: she was denied employment in the private sector because of her gender.

Shotwell's success story is all the more remarkable in that she was a minority (African American) and disabled, confined to a wheelchair because of childhood polio. A tireless activist against discrimination of any kind, she was arrested outside the Peoria City Hall in 1969 during a civil rights protest.

Born in Denver, Colorado, in 1922, Shotwell credited her family for not allowing her to use her disability as a handicap. "I was very fortunate that my family did not take care of me. They encouraged me to go to school even though they were criticized for making 'poor' Odette attend school. At that time, it was thought that people like me should be stored somewhere."

She would eventually serve as a senior chemist at the USDA

research center. In 1980 her research team received the Distinguished Service Award for "contributing to the protection of human health [by] excluding mold toxins from cereal foods, milk and animal feeds." Shotwell died in 1998.

The U.S. Department of Agriculture isn't known for its marketing savvy, but it pulled one out of the hat for Mary Ollidene Weaver. When she and her colleagues at the department's Peoria research center formulated an incredible ingredient that was capable of absorbing hundreds of times its own weight in water, there was one big problem. It's name was one that only a scientist could love (or understand): saponified starch-graft poly acrylonitrile copolymers. The USDA renamed it "Super Slurper."

Since its introduction in 1973, Super Slurper has found commercial life in products as varied as seed coats, wound dressings, automobile fuel filters, and plastic mesh barriers used at construction sites. Indeed, low-cost, lightweight disposable diapers would not have been possible without the basic technology of Super Slurper.

The invention led Weaver and her colleagues—team leader Bill Doane, Edward B. Bagley, and George F. Fanta—to win the 1977 Inventor of the Year Award by the Intellectual Property Owners. (Ollidene was the first woman recipient of the prestigious award.) They also received the USDA Distinguished Service Award and the IR 100 Award from *Industrial Research* magazine. As co-inventor, Weaver shares credit on four patents related to the product.

The technology behind Super Slurper is actually a marriage between a naturally occurring substance, starch—specifically cornstarch—and synthetic polymers. The compound's amazing absorptive quality immediately caught the eye of the private sector, stimulating thousands of inquiries nationwide. The USDA has granted forty nonexclusive licenses to make, use, or sell Super Slurper.

One of the more recognizable applications of Super Slurper technology was the development in 1992 of a biodegradable, resilient-fill packaging material—the familiar "packing peanuts." The manufacturer, Uni-Star, produces 20,000 pounds of packing peanuts a week and projects that the U.S. packaging market could easily use 254 millions pounds annually.

An activist in her own right, Weaver was a leader in organizing her peers at the research unit under the American Federation of

Government Employees union. Her colleague of fifteen years, Bill Sloane, recalls her as a consummate scientist: hardworking, dedicated, and a bit of a perfectionist.

Sloane also knew Odette Shotwell and Allene Jeanes, and he has his own idea why so many accomplished women chemists found a home in Peoria: "The center allowed a good deal of independence. If you were strong-willed and talented and wanted to make a contribution to society, they gave you the opportunity. This was a place where you could make your mark in life."

Nicole Maxwell
HERBAL REMEDIES

Society debutante, ballet dancer, journalist, adventurer, herbalist, ethnologist, author, and ecologist, Nicole Maxwell had accomplished several lifetimes' worth of work when she died at age ninety-two in 1998. However, what promises to be her most important legacy—popular acceptance of the medicinal herbs that she introduced to the Western world—eluded her to the end, as she predicted. "As soon as I'm gone," she once told a friend, "they'll come running."

In 1961 Maxwell wrote a groundbreaking book, *Witch Doctor's Apprentice*, based on decades of work in the jungles of the upper Amazon Basin. Befriending the local medicine men, she gradually learned the secrets of the indigenous tribes' herbs, meticulously cataloging their properties. These herbal cures for virtually every known ailment—from kidney stones to tooth decay—were hailed as a major work of ethnomedicine.

(Maxwell's book is known as much for its wit as its utility. In one story she tells how during one of her initial forays into the jungle, she suffered greatly from mosquito bites. She had heard that putting nail polish on the bites helped, so she dotted herself with the only color she had—bright red. When she arrived for her meeting with a very learned medicine man, he was immediately impressed by her "war paint.")

To say she was an unlikely candidate for adventurer and medical innovator is to seriously understate the case. She was born into an upper-crust San Francisco family just after the great earthquake, and

Maxwell's greatest achievement as a young woman was making her debut into high society. As was the custom of the day among upper-class children, Maxwell crossed the Atlantic in *Titanic* fashion to take a grand European tour. When she arrived in Paris, however, she never left, and she became the toast of the town in the 1920s. Elegant and lithe, she danced ballet with the Paris Opéra, posed nude for artists, and dallied with a coterie of admirers.

In 1933 Maxwell made the first of a series of abrupt direction changes in her life. She fell in love with and married an Air Force officer. Twelve years later she divorced her then–brigadier general husband and fled to Bolivia. (She later explained that since she had never been attracted to Latin men, she hoped to avoid distracting entanglements.) Looking for something to do with her life, the wealthy but bored Mrs. Maxwell became a correspondent at large for the *Lima Times*.

It was while on assignment in the jungles outside of Quito, Ecuador, that she became fascinated with medical herbs. Hacking through dense vegetation, she suffered a deep machete gash on her arm. As she pondered whether she might bleed to death, her Indian guide ran off into the jungle. To her relief, he returned with a thick, dark red tree sap, which she drank. The profuse bleeding quickly stopped, and remarkably, her ugly wound healed without a scar. (That remedy would be later described on page 103 of her book: "This tree known as sangre de drago, scientific name *Croton lechleri eurphorbiaceae*, yields a hemostatic sap that accelerates wound healing.") Her life's mission became apparent: bring the wonders of ancient herbal remedies to the modern world.

Maxwell had enough background in biology to make sense of the contradictions and superstitions that surrounded the herbal remedies. In 1958 her interest in the medicinal properties of these herbs was seemingly validated when she obtained a small grant from a U.S. drug company to collect data and plant specimens.

She returned to the States with dozens of specimens and notebooks full of remedies, including what she said was a highly effective herbal contraceptive. To her chagrin, she learned that her corporate benefactor had viewed her project as a publicity stunt; it had no real scientific interest in her work. Determined not to let her findings go unheard, she wrote a book and found a publisher.

In thirty years of research Maxwell collected 350 plants used to treat more than a hundred common maladies. She never attempted to patent a formula or make a penny from her work. She achieved guru status among an international group of admirers, who made pilgrimages to her compound in Iquitos, Peru. Though her work continued to be shunned by pharmaceutical companies, the rising popularity of herbal remedies and homeopathy in the late 1980s reinvigorated interest in her findings. Her book was republished in 1990, and she devoted much of her later years to calling attention to the destruction of the upper Amazon rain forest.

Maxwell's goal was to create a multibillion-dollar industry for South America, fueled by indigenous medical herbs instead of slash-and-burn farming. Though this dream eluded her, "she remained confident that her work would be eventually recognized by science," according to her *New York Times* obituary. At the time of her death she was collaborating with a Mississippi State University scientist on a manual of Amazonian remedies.

Dorothy Kucik
NONPOLLUTING MARINE OIL FILTER

If you've ever been close to a picturesque boat marina, then you know its beauty is superficial. The water typically is so polluted that swimming is out of the question. That's because removing a traditional marine oil filter spills about a quart of oil directly into the water. Dorothy Kucik and her husband, Michael, avid boaters themselves, developed a filter with a valve that allows the residual oil to be drained before removal.

One quart of oil can pollute a million gallons of water. Used motor oil and filters are a threat to wildlife and a safety hazard; the coast guard can fine boaters up to $5,000 for spills.

"We always tried to change the filter with a plastic bag to catch the oil," Dorothy says, "but it's difficult because of the cramped quarters in a boat engine and because once the oil spills, it sticks to the plastic bag."

The Kuciks' invention (Patent #5,366,400) is ingeniously simple.

By adding an extra valve to the bottom of the filter, a hose can be attached to drain the oil safely into a container.

Given that Americans buy millions of disposable marine filters annually, the Kuciks should be sitting on a pot of gold. But the manufacturers of the filters, whom they have approached, simply are not interested in spending the research and development money to replace the existing, albeit defective, product.

Discouraged but not defeated, the Kuciks plan to develop the product themselves. "The Coast Guard love the idea, so we're going to get it on the market if we have to manufacture it ourselves," says Michael.

Judy A. Samelson
RECYCLABLE HANDBAG

"It looks sort of like a cross between an Armani and a Chanel," says Judy A. Samelson, a former psychotherapist, of her patented handbag design. Of course, Giorgio Armani and Coco Chanel never worked with plastic bottles as purse material.

Samelson came up with idea after taking a course at the Rhode Island School of Design. A devoted environmentalist, her goal was to wed bio-friendly technology with high fashion. "A lot of items out there made of recycled material are quite homely," she says.

Samelson envisions an entire product line made by her Boston-based Recycle Design. For the time being, though, she's quite satisfied at coming pretty darn close to making the proverbial silk purse out of a sow's ear. She received Patent #5,464,108 for her invention.

Margarita Centeno
MARWOOD

Every day the population of the Philippines increases by four thousand, exacerbating the already critical housing shortage and, in turn, adding new pressure to deplete the country's rapidly diminishing forests. Margarita Centeno thought the solution was obvious: build homes from a renewable, readily available resource—trash.

In 1988 the twenty-seven-year-old resident of Manila invented Marwood, a woodlike building material made from dry leaves and plastic refuse. Dried leaves are pulverized and mixed with a glue made from melted Styrofoam and plastic in a two-to-one ratio. Because the material can be molded and is fire-resistant, it can be used for things besides building construction, such as bags, cartons, and even clogs.

In 1990 the invention won a gold medal at an international contest sponsored by the World Intellectual Property Organization. Says Centeno, "You can learn anything if you really want to."

Edith M. Flanigen
MOLECULAR FILTERS

World production of gasoline would be less efficient and more polluting without the contribution of Edith Flanigen. The holder of 102 patents and creator of more than 200 synthetic substances—mainly in the field of petroleum research and development—she is one of the most inventive chemists of all time.

Her specialty is "molecular sieves," or crystal compounds with molecule-size pores that are used to separate constituent parts of complex mixtures. These minute filters are used in water purification and environmental cleanup.

A second group of these substances serves as catalysts to accelerate chemical reactions. One of her patented catalysts, zeolite Y, is used extensively to make gasoline from crude oil.

Dr. Inge Russell
SUPERYEAST

A microbiologist at Canadian beer giant Labatt Brewing Company, Inge Russell was working in search of—what else?—a better brew when she inadvertently created a patented new life form. Although admittedly her "superyeast" produced a "terrible beer," it is capable of producing large quantities of fuel alcohol.

The superyeast was created using biotechnology. Russell fused two strains of existing yeast—one that produces beer and another that produces fuel alcohol. What makes superyeast so special is its unique ability to ferment starch, which a normal yeast cannot.

For nations like Brazil that depend on fuel alcohol made from starches such as corn or cassava, Russell's superyeast could have immediate implications. For countries like the United States, that have hesitated to invest in clean-burning alcohol fuel technology, the savings derived from using superyeast may one day lessen reliance on fossil fuels.

Today Russell directs her company's new-technology and innovation department. "My job is essentially to find ways to make everyone—at every level—more innovative and to create pathways for new ideas to bubble to the top." Though no longer full-time in research, she continues to oversee the R&D work of two Ph.D. candidates. "We have several patents pending, but of course those are trade secrets," she says.

Lori A. Todd
POLLUTANT SCANNER

Before Professor Lori Todd came along, determining pollutants in the air was an ephemeral process. Technicians would sweep the air with handheld meters, hoping to obtain enough samples to get a picture of the types and the degree of toxins. Typically the sample analysis would take a week or longer, by which time the contaminants' path could have changed radically. The technology offered only an environmental snapshot, while in fact what was needed was a motion picture.

"People would take very quick measurements over a short period of time and use them to make guesses or judgments about what's going on over the long term," she says. "My research is akin to X rays—the fancy X rays that are used in CAT scans. However, instead of shooting many rays at different angles to reconstruct body organs, I shoot infrared rays at many different angles to reconstruct chemical concentrations in air, in real time."

Her Environmental CAT Scanning method revolutionized air pollutant tracking. For the first time scientists could create a visual map of how airborne contaminants were affecting an environment. And unlike the old technology, which limited measurement to a handful of pollutants, Todd's Environmental CAT Scanning method could detect hundreds simultaneously, since each contaminant reflects light at a different wavelength.

Todd's innovation could not have come at a better time. Before 1990 the Environmental Protection Agency required only that 7 air pollutants be tracked. In 1990 Congress mandated the EPA track 189 pollutants. Realizing the value of her work, the EPA and the National Institute for Occupational Safety and Health helped to fund her early research. However, what really carried Todd's vision to reality was a $500,000 grant from the National Science Foundation.

A faculty member of the environmental sciences and engineering department at the University of North Carolina at Chapel Hill, Todd, forty-six, finds time in between inventing and teaching to pursue her "parallel career"—sculpting. In a studio far from her university lab, she uses clays to sculpt the human figure. Her work has been shown in galleries in North Carolina, New York, Tennessee, and Ohio. "It's a different kind of creativity," she notes.

Both inventing and art require a certain degree of dreaming. "At the time my idea for the Environmental CAT Scanning sounded really crazy to a lot of people, because there wasn't equipment that could do what I wanted to have done. But to me, it sounded really neat. So I worked on the theory to see if it was possible," she says. "It was what I wanted to accomplish, so everything else just happened."

And Let's Not Forget . . .

Elizabeth Bryenton invented a fertilizer employing strains of blue and green algae that provides plants with as much nitrogen as do synthetic fertilizers. But unlike synthetic fertilizers, Bryenton's algae fertilizer requires virtually no fossil fuel to produce. . . . **Elizabeth Gross,** a biochemist at Ohio State University, has devised a "living battery," a photovoltaic cell that uses living organisms to convert sunlight into usable energy. . . . While working for Archer Daniels Midland Co. in the 1960s, chemist **Twila Paulsen** developed a high-protein flour made from soybeans, an alternative protein source that may one day be an answer to world hunger. . . . **Alexandra Finley** is a young inventor who created the award-winning Green Box, a device that allows apartment dwellers to compost kitchen scraps under their sinks. . . . Canadian **Giovanna Notarandrea** thought up a reusable greeting card that doesn't require an envelope. Her invention received an honorable mention at the first annual Environmental Invention Awards in 1991. . . . **Magdalena Villaruz** invented a power tiller that floats, for use in areas like rice fields where heavy machinery would sink. Her Tiller Turtle was rejected at an inventors' contest because one judge deemed it "impractical." By that time she had already sold a thousand of them and made her first million dollars. . . . **Pamela Cole** received Patent #5,049,002 for a "method for cleaning oil spills" that essentially solidifies the wayward waste, making cleanup easy. A special lipid (saturated fatty acid) formula is melted and mingled with the spilled oil. When it hardens, the oil comes with it. . . . **Mikie B. Catcher** also had a better idea for oil spill cleanup. Hers was an "oil disc skimmer," a double flapper-valve device for scooping it up, for which she received Patent #5,141,632. . . . Like it or not, a good deal of the world, including the United States, depends on coal as an energy source. While plentiful, coal is not a clean-burning fuel. **Lucille Markam** invented the Induco Coal Conditioner, a patented substance which makes coal burn hotter, thereby reducing air pollutants and saving 25 percent on fuel costs.

CHAPTER 6

It Took a Woman

There are some things only a woman would think of. Take Gladys Ritter, for instance, who received Patent #4,526,167 for her Expandable Jock Strap, with its "elongated soft cloth envelope for an erect male organ." This, mind you, years before guys were popping those Viagra potency pills. A man might have noticed the problem, but it took a woman to implement a solution.

Would a man have patented the Toidy Seat, the practice pads of potty training? Gertrude Muller thought it up in 1915, and her family-owned Juvenile Wood Products Company manufactured them through the 1950s.

While household and personal-care patents have in this century been a minority of the patents held by women—even in a 1923 survey they accounted for less than 50 percent of the total—women have always been particularly attuned to their own needs. In early societies women fashioned tampons and menstrual pads from moss, banana bark, and wool. Contraceptive devices have been recorded as far back as ancient Egypt. And since laws were passed in the Middle Ages forbidding a woman from making a dildo, one can assume they were making them with impunity before then. Baby diapers, brassieres, bad hair days—when you have "female troubles," you need female answers. Sometimes necessity really is the mother of invention.

Herminie Cadolle, Caresse Crosby, Ida Rosenthal
THE BRA

The late nineteenth century was not a good time for comfortable clothing. Especially not for women. As former debutante Caresse Crosby once recalled, "girlish figures were being encased in a boxlike armor of whalebone and pink cordage. The contraption ran upwards from the knee to under the armpit. If petting had been practiced in those days, it could never have gone very far."

One of the early attempts to alter this tradition of incapacity was made by a Frenchwoman named Herminie Cadolle. Born in 1845 to a family of freethinkers, Cadolle emigrated to Argentina in her twenties and began selling French lingerie there. She was sufficiently success-ful to open a shop in Paris itself by 1889, and she was sufficiently fed up with her stifling corset to create an alternative.

Named by Cadolle the *bien-être,* or "well-being," the garment—in appearance not unlike the top of a 1950s-era bathing suit—was "designed to sustain the bosom and [be] supported by the shoulders."

Caresse Crosby—then known as Mary Phelps Jacob—sold the rights to her bra patent for $1,500. (Courtesy of the National Portrait Gallery, Washington, DC/Art Resource NY)

Later Cadolle added elastic to improve the fit of her invention. She continued to operate Maison Cadolle, her lingerie shop in Paris, until her death in 1933, after which the store passed on to her daughter, Alice. Cadolle Lingerie still thrives today, serving film stars and heiresses.

The *bien-être* was unfortunately of no help to American teenager Mary Phelps "Polly" Jacob. It was prewar—World War I, that is—New York City. The vivacious upper-cruster (she called banker J. P. Morgan "Uncle Jack") was still confined to a corset, and the darn thing was showing over the décolletage of her party dress. She wanted to dance, and she could barely move.

Polly got an idea. She took two silk handkerchiefs and a length of pink ribbon and instructed her ladies' maid, Marie, to piece together an undergarment according to her direction. The modern bra was constructed on the spot.

The simple undergarment was an immediate hit with Polly's New York society friends. All the girls wanted one. "It was when a stranger from Boston wrote, enclosing a dollar . . . that I decided I had something to exploit," she later recalled. She received a patent for her "backless brassiere," as she called it, on November 3, 1914.

("Brassiere," derived from the French for "upper arm," was already a term used to describe undergarments. It had nothing to do with Phillipe de Brassiere, who claimed to have invented the bra as late as 1929. His claim was refuted in court. There are also tales of an Otto Titzling or Titzlinger, who is said to have invented the bra as early as 1912. There is no patent in that name, though; the well-named Mr. T is simply an urban myth.)

While Polly had visions of becoming a manufacturing tycoon with her invention, the sweatshop business proved too taxing for a refined young lady. She eventually sold her patent rights to the Warner Corset Company for $1,500, a sum she thought "not only adequate, but magnificent." By Polly's estimate, Warner Bra made $15 million from her invention over the next thirty years.

Polly went on to marry her childhood sweetheart, Dick Peabody (of the Peabody Museum Peabodys) and bear two children. In 1921 she met the charismatic banker-cum-poet Harry Crosby. He was a bachelor of twenty-one; she was a married woman of twenty-seven. In one of the great scandals of the day, she ran off with him to Paris.

Renamed Caresse Crosby, she and Harry started the Black Sun Press, releasing some of the first editions of James Joyce, D. H. Lawrence, and Ezra Pound.

It was the book-loving Caresse who tried to interest New York publishers in another new idea: low-cost paperbound editions small enough to carry in your coat pocket. But as receptive as America was to the backless brassiere, it was not ready for the paperback book.

Harry Crosby died tragically, a suicide, in 1929. The ever unconventional Caresse died in 1970 at the age of seventy-eight, at her castle near Rome. She said in her autobiography that she always expected to invent something wonderful again. "Perpetual motion," she insisted, "is just around the corner!"

Earthshaking as young Polly's bra was, it was not the bra we wear today. Our current two-cup model in ascending sizes is the brainchild of a pint-size Russian émigré named Ida Cohen Rosenthal. Overnight she made Caresse Crosby's backless brassiere obsolete and herself a wealthy woman in the process. But that was never her intention.

Born Ida Kaganovich in Tsarist Russia, Ida changed her name to Cohen when she fled to America in 1904. She set herself up as a seamstress in Hoboken, New Jersey, and married a nice young man named William Rosenthal.

World War I created a market for ready-to-wear clothing, and the Rosenthals thrived. By the 1920s Ida and her friend Enid Bissett ran a fashionable dress shop in Manhattan. It was there they designed the bra we know today.

The two-silk-handkerchiefs-and-a-string contraption invented by Polly Jacob was fine for young women in flapper dresses. But it didn't offer the support and shaping required by the mature figure. Ida Rosenthal knew that, and with each dress she sold, she included a cleverly contrived insert—a foundation garment of her own design that made the dresses look ever so much more flattering. After a while customers returned not for the dresses but for the inserts.

The Rosenthals scraped together $4,500 and incorporated the Maiden Form Brassiere Company in 1923. By 1938 the firm had a gross annual income of $4.5 million, a figure that would reach $40 million by the 1960s and a remarkable $400 million plus today.

It was William Rosenthal, an amateur sculptor and Maiden Form's head of production, who came up with the A, B, and C cup sizes so

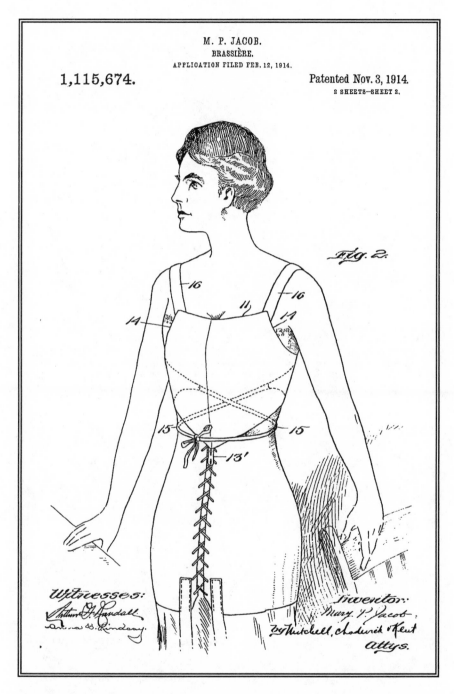

The "backless brassiere" doesn't much resemble today's scanty undies, but it was quite an improvement over the whalebone corset.

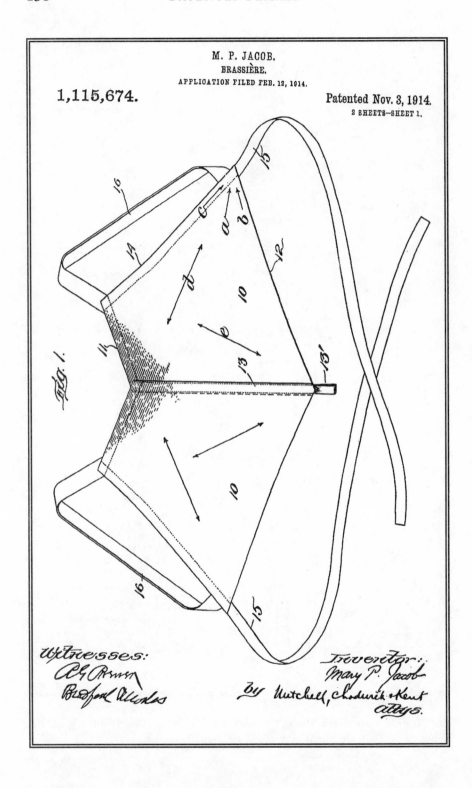

M. P. JACOB.
BRASSIÈRE.
APPLICATION FILED FEB. 12, 1914.

1,115,674.

Patented Nov. 3, 1914.
2 SHEETS—SHEET 1.

Witnesses:

Inventor:
Mary P. Jacob
by Mitchell, Chadwick & Kent
attys.

familiar today. Ida was the head of sales and marketing, traveling the world drumming up business. Eventually Maidenform (as it became known) sold its products in a hundred nations, and Ida probably visited all of them. She died in 1973 at the age of eighty-seven, handing the reins of Maidenform to her daughter.

Hinda Miller and Lisa Lindahl

JOGBRA

Ensconced in the venerable Smithsonian Institution in Washington, D.C., is an odd contraption fashioned from two jockstraps sewn together. It is the first Jogbra, and it has every reason to be enshrined there. It forever changed the way women play sports.

Breast tissue is attached to the chest wall only by a few ligaments. Constant jiggling may look good on trash TV, but it can stretch and damage tissue. Bouncing is uncomfortable, and it's unhealthy. Little wonder that sports bras are a more than $250 million annual business, comprising over 10 percent of the bra market.

We are so used to wearing these comfortable, stretchy crop tops for anything from aerobics to volleyball that it's hard to remember there was no such thing before 1977. That was when Vermont jogging enthusiasts Hinda Miller and Lisa Lindahl complained one more time that they practically had to hold their breasts steady by hand every time they went running. There should be a jockstrap for women! insisted Lisa's sister. And out of two jock straps sewn together—the very ones on display at the Smithsonian—the Jogbra was born.

Unlike many of the inventions by women over the years, the Jogbra met with almost no resistance. Miller—then twenty-seven years old with a master's degree in costume design—borrowed $5,000 from her father, and she and Lindahl got to work. They studied nineteenth-century corsets, and they deconstructed twentieth-century jockstraps. They found a small manufacturer and produced six hundred Jogbras. The first sporting goods store they visited bought the entire order: the owner's daughter, it turned out, was an avid runner.

In less than a year the Jogbra was prominently featured in running magazines and available in stores nationwide. By 1990 Jogbras were selling at the rate of eight hundred thousand annually. Miller and Lindahl sold the company that year to the bra giant Playtex for a reported $10 million. Later the product became known as the Champion Jogbra when Playtex was taken over by the $20 billion conglomerate Sara Lee. Miller stayed on as vice president of communication for the firm; Lindahl retired from both inventing and the garment business.

More recently Miller has helped Champion design a line of Jogbras for the fuller-busted athlete: "Compression doesn't work for larger women," says Miller, who helped create styles that avoid what she calls the "uniboob" look. Her advice to the aspiring inventor? "Be absolutely committed to getting the job done, regardless of what it takes."

Rommy Revson
SCUNCI

We call them "scrunchies," those ubiquitous cloth-covered rubber bands, because of the way the fabric bunches up when at rest. But it isn't a scrunchy—it's a Scunci. Inventor Rommy Revson named it after her pet Lhasa Apso puppy. More than 2 billion Scuncis have been sold in the past ten years, and it all started because of a bad divorce and a worse bleach job.

In 1987 Rommy Revson was forty years old. Revlon cosmetics heir John Revson had just divorced her, and the settlement was so ungenerous she was forced to go back to work. To that end she went out and got a brand-new hairdo . . . and emerged from the salon with a headful of straw. "It was breaking off in handfuls!" cried Revson.

With job interviews to attend, Revson needed a way to pull her hair back without pulling it out. "Rubber bands were out of the question," she said. But if she could cover the elastic with soft cloth, maybe it wouldn't snag her poor hair . . .

Revson bought a variety of fabrics to coordinate with her different outfits and taught herself to sew. When she felt she had the perfect ponytail holder, she patented the Scunci and set up meetings with hair-accessory companies. Every executive turned her down. "This is not what women want," they said.

But since every executive also happened to be male, Revson considered the source and kept at it. She took it to the women, cobbling together a small group of investors and placing ads in women's magazines. Soon she was getting more orders than she could fill.

Simplicity itself, the Scunci is incredibly easy to knock off. Revson protected her patent rights by bringing in lawyers as her business partners: the longer they protected her exclusivity, the bigger their profits. It must have worked. Last time we saw a picture of Rommy Revson, she was driving a big new Mercedes with the license plate SCUNCI.

Tomima Edmark
TOPSY TAIL

In 1992 Tomima Edmark was thirty-five years old. She was smart, she was aggressive, she was on the fast track as a marketing representative at IBM in Dallas, Texas. And then, overnight, IBM downsized, and she was out of work.

It was the best thing that ever happened to her.

What Edmark did was take her severance package and use the money to buy a television ad for an invention of hers, a hairstyling tool she called the Topsy Tail. That ad sold 3.6 million Topsy Tails, earning her company profits of more than $10 million in its first three years. By 1995 Edmark had patented half a dozen other ideas and the Topsy Tail Company had grown to an $80 million–a–year business. And it all started at the movies.

Edmark says she was waiting on line to see the romantic comedy *When Harry Met Sally . . .* and studying the attractive French braid of the woman in front of her. She found herself analyzing the complex upsweep from the inside out—probably, Edmark says, because she's dyslexic. "Would a normal person ever think to turn a ponytail inside out? I doubt it—that's a really dyslexic concept."

She knew she could duplicate that French braid quickly and easily if only she had the right tool. After dead ends made out of toothbrushes, paper clips and rubber bands, Edmark came up with a gizmo fashioned from a circular knitting needle. With a flip and a twist it turned a ponytail into a lush cascade. So simple anyone could have thought of it! But of course no one had.

Two hair-accessory manufacturers took one look at the gadget—and passed.

Edmark decided to do it herself. She went to every injection-molding company in the Dallas Yellow Pages, and they all turned her down. The Topsy Tail would never generate enough business to be worth their while, they said. Finally Edmark found one company who would—for an inflated price—take her business. She took $6,000 out of her savings account and ordered the first batch of Topsy Tails. It was 1991.

The initial ads for Topsy Tail ran in hair-care magazines, and the response was underwhelming. Initial orders totaled only $1,000, not nearly enough to keep the company afloat. Thank goodness Edmark still had her job at IBM.

Two things happened in 1992. *Glamour* magazine gave a favorable mention to the Topsy Tail. And Edmark lost her job. A million Topsy Tails later, Edmark was finally forced to hire a chief financial officer and a director of marketing. "I didn't know how big or small the company was going to be," she says, so she always kept her staff small. That way she'd never have to downsize others as she was downsized herself.

An overnight multimillionaire from her simple creation, Edmark has never stopped inventing. Among her other products are the Bowrette, which turns scarves or ribbons into attractive hair bows and the Halo, a wide-brimmed, collapsible sun hat. Thanks to her marketing savvy, a major toy manufacturer sells a My Pretty Topsy Tail doll and a major publisher features *The Topsy Tail Book* of hairstyling tips. Topsy Tails are distributed in the United States, Canada, Mexico, Europe, South Africa, and the Pacific Rim. Edmark travels fifty thousand miles and spends $100,000 a year protecting her patent in far-flung markets.

For fun, Edmark likes to go fly-fishing with her husband, and she likes to smoke cigars. In fact, she wrote a book about the latter: *Cigar Chic: A Woman's Perspective*. According to the Cigar Association of America, only about 1 percent of cigar smokers are women. According to the U.S. Patent Office, only about 8 percent of inventors are women.

Tomima Edmark has always been one to buck the percentages.

Mary Ellen Hills
Dazzle Dot

It's a simple idea and it sells for a buck, but the Dazzle Dot has been sufficiently dazzling to take Mary Ellen Hills out of husband Tony's auto repair shop and set her up as a mini-mogul. The Dazzle Dot Lipstick Mirror is selling in the six figures annually, and Hills has a few other inventions up her sleeve, as well.

It all started in 1993, when the then-thirty-eight-year-old Californian was out to dinner with her husband. She wanted to freshen her lipstick, but couldn't find a mirror in her purse. As she touched up her makeup by the reflection in a dessert spoon, she remarked, "Somebody ought to put a mirror on the end of lipstick caps." And Tony said, "Why don't you do it?"

So was born the Dazzle Dot, a little round stick-on mirror made of acrylic and sold in blister packs of two. Stick it on a lipstick, stick it on a contact lens case—instant visual feedback. Mary Ellen Hills says it took a lot of library research and the helping hand of the Service Corps of Retired Executives (SCORE) in San Francisco to bring the

Mary Ellen Hills's Dazzle Dot proved more effective than the back of a spoon . . . and much more profitable. (With kind permission of Mary Ellen Hills)

American women spend $500 million a year on lipstick. They want to see it going on. (With kind permission of Mary Ellen Hills)

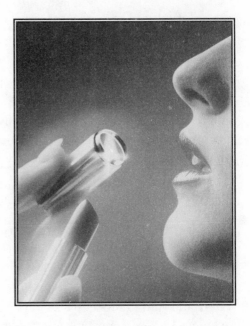

idea from inception to fruition. But it was also the right idea at any time. After all, women spend half a *billion* dollars a year on lipstick. They want to see it going on. (On the other hand, Susan Natali's Brush Mirror—patent #D306,523—while good in concept, is frequently on the wrong side of your head when you want to look into it.)

Today Mary Ellen's business has pretty much squeezed out the auto repair shop, what with a full-time employee and a raft of independent sales reps, all those orders to fill and checks to cash. Tony isn't complaining.

Dr. Judith Esser-Mittag

O.B. TAMPON

How often did we hear that television commercial tagline throughout the seventies and eighties: "Designed by a *woman* gynecologist"? Johnson & Johnson was trying to sell us on the fact that the o.b. brand tampon was superior to the competition because someone intimately familiar with female anatomy had put it together.

They were right, of course.

The woman gynecologist who designed the o.b. tampon—that little teeny one without the cardboard tube—was Dr. Judith Esser-Mittag, a German physician. And she actually invented the o.b. back in 1950 in Germany, when she was a lowly medical resident.

Dr. Esser (later to marry lawyer Heinz Mittag) was barely out of Cologne University medical school when she first went to work as a consultant for the Carl Hahn Company, manufacturers of feminine hygiene products. She was still a resident at the Women's State Hospital in Wuppertal until 1951. But from 1947 to 1950 she did the studies on female anatomy and menstrual microbiology that led her to construct the cotton-rayon innovation. The tampon was smaller and more body friendly than earlier models, needing no bulky applicator. Carl Hahn began to market the o.b. in 1950, and it remained a wholly European idea for two decades.

It wasn't until the consumer giant Johnson & Johnson bought the Carl Hahn Company in 1973 that the o.b. was introduced to the American buyer. By 1974 it was imported in large quantities from Germany; by 1976 it was being manufactured in Sherman, Texas, at a Johnson & Johnson plant. It made an immediate, if modest, impact on the menses industry. Most memorable were those earnest TV commercials.

Dr. Esser-Mittag stayed closely associated with the product she created. She consulted with J&J when they introduced o.b. to America; she even took questions from consumers on an o.b. hotline. Later, during the toxic shock syndrome scare, she testified in court about the medical implications of tampon use and the safety and efficacy of her design.

Dr. Esser-Mittag is officially retired now, but still much in demand as a lecturer. Her specialty is adolescents: educating girls and young women about their bodies, female health care, and reproductive medicine.

Sarah Breedlove "Madam C. J." Walker
Hair Relaxer

Sarah Breedlove was born in a Louisiana sharecropper's shack in December 1867, the first free child in a family of emancipated slaves. Orphaned at the age of six, she was married by the time she was

BLACK HERITAGE

32
USA

Madam C. J. Walker

Sarah Breedlove Walker went from a sharecropper's shack to a mansion on the Hudson to a U.S. postage stamp.

fourteen, a mother at seventeen, and widowed by the time she was twenty. Yet when she was forty-six, she had become America's first black millionaire and the first self-made woman millionaire.

What she invented was Wonderful Hair Grower, a conditioner for African American hair that promoted a healthy shine and relaxed tight curls. The formula, she always said, came to her in a dream, and she mixed up the first batches in her washtubs. Because before Sarah became Madam C. J. Walker, one of the largest employers of African American women in the country, she was a laundress.

It was probably the stress, hard work, and alkaline fumes from her work as a washerwoman that made Sarah's hair fall out. After she mixed up her potion and her hair grew back in, she became her own best advertisement. By 1905 the self-named "Madam C. J." (such titles prevented whites from condescendingly addressing blacks by their first names) was training Walker Agents all over the Midwest in how to give black women the fashionable hairdos of the day, using pomades, hot combs, and curlers. Walker did, in fact, invent an improved hot comb.

By 1911 the Walker Company boasted a sales force of 950 women, all neatly and recognizably dressed in starched white shirts and long black skirts. By 1918 the concern was earning $250,000 a year. In its heyday the Walker Company (of which Madam C. J. was sole stockholder and president for life) fielded 3,000 Walker Agents around the country. In that era being a Walker Agent was an African American woman's best shot at comfortable self-support. The Walker Way spread as far as Paris, when American singer Josephine Baker adopted the signature look and began an international fad.

Firmly established and finally secure, Madam C. J. became a philanthropist, patron of the arts, and civil rights activist, even meeting with President Woodrow Wilson in 1917 to argue her cause. She died a hero to her people in 1919 at the age of fifty-one, leaving the Walker Company to her daughter, A'Lelia. The Walker Building in Indianapolis, Indiana, now operating as the nonprofit Walker Urban Life Center, still stands, a tribute to someone who overcame the odds.

Marjorie Joyner

PERMANENT WAVING MACHINE

Madam C. J. Walker's most valued employee, Marjorie Joyner, holds Patent #1,693,515 for her 1928 invention of the "Permanent Waving Machine." It's that strange apparatus we still see parodied in cartoons, where wires are clamped onto sections of hair, a metal hood is lowered onto the poor client's head, and electricity is zapped into each curl.

This permanent wave machine may look like a joke, but it actually worked beautifully. (©1938 by Consumers Union of U.S., Inc., Yonkers, NY 10703-1057, a nonprofit organization. Reprinted with permission from Consumer Reports *for educational purposes only. No commercial use or photocopying permitted. Log onto www.ConsumerReports.org.)*

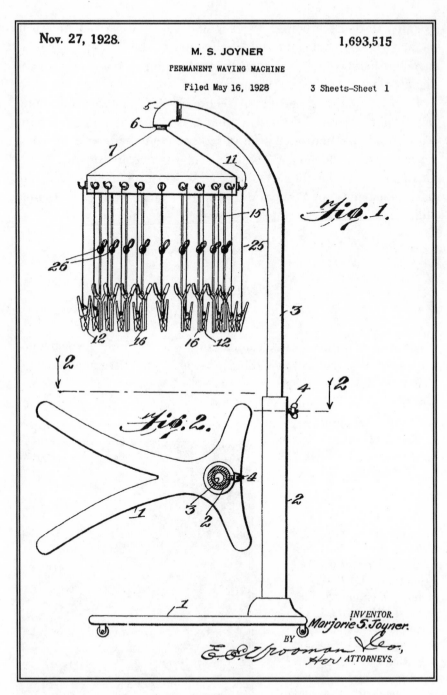

It was Madam C.J. Walker's company that received the profits from Marjorie Joyner's invention.

The thing is—it works. The curls looked better and lasted longer than any other method available at the time produced.

As Joyner told historian Anne MacDonald in 1991, "We operators would put in a very nice hairdo, but . . . in the morning, a customer who looked beautiful when she left my care looked like an accident going someplace to happen!"

Joyner was one of the thousands of African American women who went to work for the Walker Company in the 1920s. She knew that for black women more than anyone, "people need to make their own opportunities, and appearance is important. A good personal appearance helps people get and hold jobs." By helping others get jobs, she herself became the director of the late Madam Walker's nationwide chain of beauty schools. Unfortunately, she invented her device while in its employ, and the Walker Company got all the profits.

In 1945 Joyner cofounded the United Beauty School Owners and Teachers Association. Honored by the *Washington Post* as the "Grande Dame of Black Beauty Culture," she died in 1995 at the age of ninety-eight, respected and beloved.

Marion Donovan

Disposable Diaper

Surprise—a woman invented the disposable diaper. After all, who else *needed* it more?

It was 1950, and the Baby Boom was a pig in the population python. Marion Donovan was just like every other young wife and mother in suburban New York: inundated with dirty diapers. Diapers that needed to be washed, bleached, twice rinsed, and hung out to dry. There had to be an easier way!

Out of a shower curtain and absorbent cotton padding, Donovan created what she called the Boater: a disposable diaper with a snap-on, leak-resistant cover. She patented it in 1951 and went around to New York–area manufacturers in an attempt to sell her idea.

The manufacturers to whom she took her prototype were notably unimpressed. The Boater was too expensive, they said. No one was going to pay good money for a product they were just going to throw away. Notably, most of these manufacturers were men.

In the end, Donovan self-financed production of the Boater. She brought the product to area department stores, and it was soon flying off the shelves. Eventually Donovan sold her firm for $1 million, and low-cost disposable diapers soon became a supermarket staple.

Donovan went on to invent a skirt hanger that holds up to thirty items and an elasticized zipper pull.

And Let's Not Forget . . .

Ruth Handler, inventor of the Barbie doll, later in life invented the Nearly Me natural breast prosthesis after undergoing a mastectomy. . . . **Isabelle Budd** of Ottawa, Canada, holds a patent on the Double Breast Prosthesis, a lightweight camisole insert. . . . A disfiguring birthmark led **Lydia O'Leary** to formulate the supercoverage makeup called Covermark. She became the first person granted a patent for a cosmetic when she proved its usefulness by washing it off in front of the panel of judges, revealing the wine-colored blotch underneath. . . . Former flamenco dancer **Chips Klein,** unable to properly apply eyeliner in makeshift dressing rooms, invented the Eye Maker three-way makeup mirror. . . . Jewelry designer **Victoria Tane** came up with Headbenz, "a completely adjustable headband that won't give you a headache." . . . **Angie Beck,** along with her husband, Bruce, received patent #5,411,034 for a condom that changes color when it breaks or tears. . . . Early African American innovator **Beatrice Kenner** bucked the odds by inventing back in the 1920s (an adjustable sanitary belt), and was still at it in 1987 (a shower-mounted back scrubber). . . . **Jane Hunnicut** designed the Reality Condom, the first mass-marketed (although to poor reception) female condom. . . . **Dr. Ethel Grene** developed a seat belt for pregnant women. . . . And for the woman driving alone, **Barbara LesStrang** built Safe-T Man, a life-size male mannequin ready to serve and protect—or, at least, look like he was. (Not recommended for use in carpool lanes!)

CHAPTER 7

Women in Space

The name of the Pathfinder should be Sojourner Truth . . . because she was a heroine to Blacks, slaves and women. She acted on her strong feelings about life and the way it should be. . . . She went on many journeys and told many truths [so] it's very logical that the Pathfinder be named Sojourner Truth because it is on a journey to find truths about Mars."

So wrote elementary school student Valerie Ambrose of Bridgeport, Connecticut, in her letter to the Jet Propulsion Laboratory. Valerie's proposal was selected by the scientists and engineers of the Mars Landing Project among thirty-five hundred entries in a nationwide contest to name the Mars rover. The fact that the vehicle was invented by a woman (Donna Shirley) and named after a woman by a young woman is affirmation that gender barriers have fallen in the fields of aeronautic engineering and space sciences.

In truth, the skies and the stars have fascinated women throughout history. Hypatia of Alexandria (A.D. 370–412), the earliest woman scientist whose life is documented, invented the astrolabe, a device that could calculate the position of the sun and the constellations. German astronomer Caroline Herschel discovered eight comets by 1797 and helped to establish, with her brother William, the field of modern astronomy. She received gold medals from the kings of Great Britain and Prussia for her work.

The world's first air force commander was a woman: Madame

Blanchard was appointed by Emperor Napoleon Bonaparte to be his chief air minister of ballooning in 1804. A century later, when the brothers Wright made history at Kitty Hawk, sister Katharine Wright was by their side. Though not a pilot herself, she was considered the third member of the Wright team. She ran the business side of their aviation company and through her savvy successfully defended several patent suits.

In 1911, barely five years after Kitty Hawk, Harriet Quimby became the first woman pilot. An editor for the popular magazine *Leslie's Illustrated Weekly*, she set her sights on challenging the existing belief that women lacked the stamina needed to fly. She disguised herself as a man, took flying lessons, and then wrote about the experience. She was so enthralled with flying that she began working as a daredevil pilot, dressed in a signature purple satin flying suit. Tragically, she died in an air show over Boston in July 1912.

Throughout the 1920s and 1930s, women aviators were defying stereotypes and barnstorming their way through aeronautical history. Amelia Earhart quashed the notion of male air superiority when she set the transatlantic world speed record in 1932. Louise Thaden became the first woman to win the prestigious Bendix Race in 1935. Jackie Cochran set three speed records and a world altitude record of thirty-three thousand feet—all before 1940. (By the time of her death in 1980, she held more speed and altitude records than anyone in the world, male or female.)

While women pilots were restricted to noncombat missions during World War II, no such restriction was placed on women aeronautics engineers. Canadian Elsie MacGill transformed a railway boxcar plant into an airplane factory and supervised the production of twenty-three Hawker Hurricane Fighters per week for the Allied effort. Irmgard Flugge-Lotz, Germany's answer to MacGill, was a captive warrior who, in 1953 as an American citizen, made the development of jet aircraft possible with her invention of automatic flight control.

In the 1950s astronomy, rocketry, computer science, aeronautical engineering, and other applied sciences all merged to form the foundation of Soviet and American space programs. Today you will find women at the forefront of technology and discovery in all areas of the space sciences. No doubt Hypatia, Sojourner, Madame Blanchard, and Amelia—not to mention young Valerie—would be pleased.

Donna Shirley
MARS ROVER

The story of Donna Shirley begins with a small-town girl from Oklahoma who found herself hopelessly starstruck by age twelve. Nothing unusual on the face of it, except that while her peers dreamed of movie stars and rock stars, Shirley dreamed of interplanetary travel to distant stars.

"Well, I got the idea that I personally wanted to go to Mars after reading Arthur C. Clarke's book *The Sands of Mars*, about colonizing Mars, and I got really fascinated with the idea. So I've wanted to go to Mars ever since," she says.

Donna Shirley and her team captured the imagination of the world when their invention, the Sojourner Truth, *rolled across Martian terrain.*

The United States Postal Service commemorated Donna Shirley and her NASA team's achievement with a stamp.

Over the July 4 weekend in 1997, she came as close as humanly possible to fulfilling her thirty-year dream as the world watched her invention, the *Sojourner Truth,* roll across the Martian terrain. As manager of NASA's Mars Explorer Program, she was on hand to lend commentary to the unprecedented events that were unfolding and that ultimately proved to be a stunning success. "I feel great. I feel terrific. It's Christmas and Fourth of July all rolled into one," she told ABC-TV's science editor, Michael Gillen.

Designed as a "mobile geologist," the six-wheel-drive Mars rover was the first vehicle to autonomously traverse another planet. For two years Shirley and her team of scientists and engineers at NASA's Jet Propulsion Laboratory in Pasadena, California, labored over (and this was Shirley's brainstorm) a twenty-two-pound robot the size of a microwave oven. A host of skeptical colleagues "said it could not be done," she now recalls with some relish.

Data collected from the *Sojourner Truth* is still being analyzed, but almost immediately it provided solid evidence that water once flowed across the Red Planet. Pictures beamed back to Earth showed stream beds strewn with rocks and boulders, much like a dry wash in the American Southwest.

The origin of the *Sojourner* project is a testament not only to Shirley's feminine ingenuity but also to her well-honed management skills. She came to JPL in 1966 and began working on a Mars landing in 1971. The landing never happened, because the project was canceled by Congress. In the late eighties, when the agency was again flush with cash, the Mars project was resuscitated, and work began on the planetary rovers. They were the size of pickup trucks and came complete with rockets to return the vehicles and rock samples back to Earth.

At the time Shirley was chief engineer of a $1.6 billion project to explore asteroids, a comet, and Saturn when she was given the nod in 1991 to head up the Mars project. By then the budget for the Mars mission had ballooned to $10 billion, and no one was willing to fund it. The main problem was the cost of the rocketry needed to haul the oversize rover around the solar system. While her male colleagues were ready to scrap the whole project, Shirley suggested that perhaps size was not important in all cases. Could not the one-eighth-scale prototype of the rover become the vehicle itself? And *Sojourner* was born.

Shirley herself was born in Wynnewood, Oklahoma (population 2,000), in 1942. A self-proclaimed tomboy, when it came time to choose a high school elective, she opted for mechanical drawing over home economics. Father was the town physician, and Mother was a preacher's daughter and society matron who demanded perfectionism in her daughter. By the time she was sixteen, Donna was already realizing her ambitions by learning to fly an airplane.

She earned bachelor degrees in professional writing and aerospace engineering from the University of Oklahoma, and after beginning work at JPL, went to night school at the University of Southern California to graduate with a master's degree in aerospace engineering in 1968. She's currently working on her Ph.D., while continuing her full-time job at JPL. She's also a full-time mom to daughter Laura Diane (she and her husband, a JPL laser and propulsion researcher, divorced after twenty years of marriage in 1993).

Shirley called upon her writing skills in 1998 to coauthor a book with *People* magazine correspondent Danelle Morton about her experiences heading up the Mars landing project. One comes away from reading *Managing Martians* feeling that Shirley would have made a great CEO or military leader had she not stuck to the stars. Her ability to maintain her cool under tremendous stress—slashed budgets, impossible deadlines, gut-wrenching rivalries with peers—is as much a lesson for bureaucratic managers as it is for science buffs. Indeed, she has another book waiting in the wings: *Managing Creativity*, which describes her nonlinear management style.

The Mars Exploration Program is far from over; robotic flying missions have been scheduled to Mars every twenty-six months for at least the next decade. Next up is an exploration of the Red Planet's polar regions, which hopes to answer the next big question: what happened to Mars's water? But, truth be told, Shirley is starting to get itchy feet. "For years, I could think of nothing better than managing a flight to Mars. Now I've done it, and I'm ready for something else."

Venus, anyone?

Ellen Ochoa
OPTICAL IMAGING

When astronaut Ellen Ochoa recently participated in a live Internet chat with students at elementary schools across the country, the most popular question was "How do you go to the bathroom?" Ochoa, a Ph.D. in electrical engineering from Stanford University, was unfazed. She patiently explained there is indeed a toilet on the space shuttle *Discovery*, but "we depend on airflow instead of gravity to get rid of the waste."

All in a day's work for a scientist who wears several hats (including a space helmet) at NASA's Lyndon B. Johnson Space Center in Houston.

When she's not flying space missions (a total of 484 hours in space), Ochoa serves as a spacecraft communicator in Mission Control. She is the former chief of the Intelligence Systems Technology Branch, supervising thirty-five engineers and scientists in the research and development of computational systems for aerospace missions. And she is a co-inventor on three patents for an optical inspection system, an optical object-recognition method, and a method for noise removal in images.

Born May 10, 1958, in Los Angeles, Ochoa holds the distinction of being the first Latina astronaut, but she seriously contemplated a career other than science. "When I first went to college, my plan was to major in music or business, so you can see I veered off that path considerably," she says, although she continues today with her amateur pursuit as a classical flutist.

"It wasn't really until I was in graduate school that I decided to try to get selected as an astronaut. The first women astronauts were chosen when I was in college, so before that it never seemed like something I would be able to do. I found out from some graduate school friends about the application process and realized I would be eligible to apply when I got my doctorate, and I did. It was five years later when I was actually selected," she says.

She became an astronaut in July 1991 and subsequently has flown two separate space shuttle flights. During the first nine-day mission, in April 1993, she and the other crew members of *Discovery* conducted studies on the effects of solar activity on the Earth's climate and environment. One of her primary tasks was controlling the Remote Manipulator System (RMS), a robotic arm, to deploy and capture the *Spartan* satellite, which studied the solar corona.

On November 3, 1994, she began an eleven-day mission as the payload commander of the *Discovery*'s atmospheric laboratory for applications and science. Again she used the RMS to retrieve another research satellite at the end of its eight-day free flight.

She has vivid memories from both experiences. "The most challenging aspect was all the information we had to learn, and be able to remember it, to support a shuttle flight. We needed to know how all the shuttle systems worked—including the life support, propulsion, computers, communications, mechanical systems, et cetera."

On the lighter side, she recalls that *Discovery* was the definitive room with a view. "One of the more interesting views was of Hurricane Florence and Typhoon Zelda, which both formed during my second flight. It's amazing to see a storm start small, then build to a very big size over several days, with a well-defined eye in the middle."

One of her recent assignments back on terra firma was serving as the director of the Astronaut Office for the International Space Station program, training new crews in safety, procedures, and robotics.

"I hope that my future involvement will be as a crew member on a shuttle mission assembling the International Space Station," said Ochoa in a 1997 interview. "It will take four to five years to complete, but the first crew will arrive about six months after we begin assembly."

The multinational project is evidence of a maturing space program, says Ochoa. "I think the world has changed considerably between when we first started going into space and now. During the race to the moon it was seen as a competition in many ways. It helped to obtain funding, but overall it was probably not the best reason to do it. When we actually made it to the moon, the program was over, and we weren't able to take advantage of our success by doing a lot of science.

"Now we are learning to work together on programs that we can all support and that will benefit people all around the world."

Alice Chatham, Bernadette Luna
SPACE SUIT

When Alice Chatham created one-of-a-kind designs for the stars in the 1950s, it had nothing to do with the golden era of Hollywood. As an employee of the air force and later NASA, she handmade the helmet worn by Chuck Yeager when he first broke the sound barrier, and she went on to design space helmets for the astronauts. Today research engineer Bernadette Luna is carrying on Chatham's work at NASA, but she uses computers to design life-support and space-suit technology to be used in the twenty-first century.

A well-known sculptor in Dayton, Ohio, Alice King Chatham had worked on special assignment during World War II to design a leakproof rubber mask for fighter plane pilots. Reasoned the air force scientists, who knew more about the human exterior than a sculptor?

In 1947 Chatham was approached again by the air force to participate on the top-secret X-1 project—the world's first rocket plane. Her mission: find a way to protect the test pilot from the enormous pressure encountered at an altitude of one hundred thousand feet. Her solution was the world's first pressurized flight helmet.

Her design consisted of a full-face rubber mask attached to a cloth hood, which was pressurized by means of an inflatable rubber "bladder" that also covered the ears. It was crude by today's standards, but it did the trick.

Chatham went on to create state-of-the-art headgear for space travel, first for test animals and later for the original seven astronauts of the Mercury project. Along the way she added to her list of NASA inventions the first pressurized space suit, stretch-knit undergarments for astronauts, a space bed, and various tethering devices.

As a research engineer specializing in life-support technologies, Bernadette Luna is part of a bioengineering team that has one foot in the research lab and the other in the Astronaut Office. "Since the astronauts are the eventual users of our products, I get a firsthand account of what space flight is like," she says.

Her particular assignment focuses on NASA's future missions, and developing a new generation of space suits, she must consider mechanical design, physiology, thermal analysis, and computer programming. Since the job is in effect half biology and half engineering, her technologies have a dual use, and some have been adopted for medical life-support systems.

The mother of three visits local schools several times each year to talk about her work at NASA "My advice is you *can* have a career and family and still be happy. The women who are doing both now are pioneering the way, pushing for flexible work options that someday will be commonplace."

The Discoverers

Not every good idea or innovation is patentable. The definition of a patent has broadened over the years—as late as the 1920s there was no such thing as a medical patent. The first patent for computer software was granted in the 1950s. Today techniques, therapies, and methodologies are patentable.

But unless something can be translated into a product or device, the Patent and Trademark Office is unlikely to award a patent to a discovery. So the following group of extraordinary women will have to be satisfied that their findings have significantly advanced earth and space sciences.

Jocelyn Bell
THE PULSAR

Jocelyn Bell was a postgraduate student in 1967 when she discovered an entirely new celestial phenomenon. Thirty years after its discovery, the pulsar is still too new for scientists to understand all its ramifications, but many believe that pulsars hold clues to the beginnings of the universe.

At the time of her discovery, Bell was analyzing literally miles of printouts from an enormous radio telescope built under the direction of Professor Anthony Hewish of England's Cambridge University to study another celestial phenomenon, the quasar. As she scanned through the data, she began to notice radio signals too fast and regular to come from quasars. She and Hewish determined that the signals must be coming from rapidly spinning, superdense collapsed stars. The media coined the term "pulsar" for these pulsating stars.

Bell's findings were initially greeted with disbelief. Eventually Hewish alone received the Nobel Prize for the discovery of the pulsar, although Bell would go on to be acknowledged with many other medals and awards from American and British scientific bodies. Today a respected professor in her own right, Bell recently delivered a lecture entitled "Neutron Stars, Einstein and Nobel" in which she discussed how neutron stars can allow for precise testing of Einstein's General Theory of Relativity.

Roberta Score
EXTRATERRESTRIAL LIFE

In 1984 Roberta Score was manager of the Antarctic meteor lab at the Johnson Space Center when she flew to the South Pole as part of a fact-finding mission. Searching the Allan Hills of the remote southern tip of the Antarctic continent, she discovered the 4.5 billion-year-old meteorite that scientists believe may contain the first evidence of life beyond Earth.

"It was shortly after Christmas Day, and we were heading out in this area in which the only rocks you saw were meteorites. There were no terrestrial rocks around. And this particular area had these things called pinnacles, which are basically these spectacular ice sculptures twelve to fifteen feet high. Just as we were leaving, I ran into this particular rock," Score recalled in a recent interview on National Public Radio.

The rock, about the size of a cantaloupe, appeared to be very green. Ironically, that turned out to be an optical illusion, the blue arctic light playing tricks on the eyes. Back in the lab the rock was a dull gray. Cataloged ALH84001 (ALH for Allan Hills), the rock was classified as having a somewhat common composition, and that was the end of the story. Or so everyone believed.

Ten years later a former classmate of Score's was doing routine analysis on the meteorites and discovered that the rock was Martian. This in and of itself is extraordinary: there are only twelve known Martian meteorites. But there was something even more special about ALH84001. "This is the oldest, and it's just totally different from any others," said Score.

It's estimated to have formed on Mars 4.5 billion years ago, before being blasted into space in a trajectory toward earth about 16 million years ago.

Two years later, in 1996, further analysis revealed that the ancient Martian rock contained minute objects called polycyclic aromatic hydrocarbons (PAHs). These closely resemble fossilized bacteria found on Earth. Not everyone believes this theory; another group of scientists contends that the PAHs were deposited within the rock by meltwater from surrounding ice. Nonsense, say Score and her colleagues. The surrounding ice doesn't contain PAHs.

The focus of Score's work continues to be Antarctica. Although profiles in *People* magazine and interviews on TV have considerably raised her media profile since that fateful day in 1984, she remains modest about her discovery: "It was a team effort. I hate the fact that I'm the only one getting the credit."

Luann Becker
EXTRATERRESTRIAL ORIGIN OF LIFE ON EARTH

Imagine a meteorite the size of Mount Everest hurtling toward Earth. Moments after it hits through the atmosphere, it impacts the surface with a force a thousand times greater than the energy of all the world's nuclear arsenals. That scenario (played out repeatedly in recent Hollywood disaster films) actually occurred 1.85 billion years ago. The remnants of the catastrophic collision can be witnessed today in an enormous crater—thirty-nine miles by nineteen miles—near Sudbury, Ontario, Canada.

In 1996 Canadian geologists sent rocks from the site to Jeffrey Bada, a geochemist with the Scripps Institute of Oceanography in San Diego, and he in turn forwarded the rocks for analysis to Luann Becker, a postdoctoral fellow serving jointly at Scripps and at NASA's Research Center in central California. Her specialty is detecting organic compounds in geochemical samples, and what she found was no less than what some scientists consider the origins of life on Earth.

The rock contained molecules of linked carbon atoms that scientists have nicknamed "buckyballs," because their structure is similar to the geodesic domes designed by architect/philosopher Buckminster Fuller. Buckyballs contain an inner cavity large enough to trap an atom. These contained an atom so rich in helium that they bore an indelible extraterrestrial signature.

The discovery of a hydrocarbon that arrived so early in Earth's development is significant because it's the first physical evidence supporting the theory that the raw materials for the origins of life were supplied from outside our planet.

"We thought we had found a clever way to study Earth's early atmosphere," said Becker in a recent interview. "Instead the buckyballs were cleverer than we were. They came right out of the stars and managed to survive an impact. I really think of them as stardust."

Andrea Ghez

PLANET-IN-FORMATION

If one could turn back the hands of time, the formation of planet Earth would have probably looked very similar to what astronomer Andrea Ghez witnessed on a still, moonlit night in May 1998. Perched before the powerful Keck Telescope at the observatory on Mauna Kea, Hawaii, she saw a dramatically warped structure in a disk surrounding star HR4796. Scientists believe this is first direct evidence of a planet actually forming around a star outside our solar system.

Until now, Ghez says, "We have based our ideas of how planets form on very little evidence. . . . We've never really seen the structure that gives rise to the planets." While astronomers have detected stellar dust disks via infrared spectrometers, the warped disk surrounding star HR4796 is probably the first actual look at the building blocks for a planet. "You're looking at the construction site. You can begin to see some of the framework going up."

The warped disk (undoubtedly someone will soon devise a catchier name for this phenomenon—planetlet? protoplanet?) is significant on another level: it's the first evidence that planets might exist in double star systems, like HR4796. Since the vast majority of most young stars are doubles (our sun is the exception to the rule), then that dramatically increases the likelihood of planets outside our solar system. Says Ghez, "Part of the fun of being at the telescope is speculating."

As a graduate student at Caltech, Ghez had already affected astronomy with her discovery that younger stars are more likely to be twins than single celestial bodies, which meant that stars are probably born double. In August 1998 she shook up the science community again in a paper delivered at Rutgers University in which she presented the best evidence yet that at the center of the Milky Way is a massive black hole.

Still, Ghez, who at thirty-six is one of UCLA's youngest tenured professors, finds some of her most rewarding work outside the observatory and in the classroom. During her undergraduate studies she founded a Big Sister program to mentor incoming women. Today she personally guides five graduate and two undergraduate students. Until women achieve equal recognition for their efforts, she feels strongly that it's important to "show the girls—and the boys—that a woman can be an astronomer."

Susan Tereby
PLANET OUTSIDE THE SOLAR SYSTEM

Ever since Jules Verne wrote about interplanetary travel in the nineteenth century, the public has been fascinated with the possibility. Indeed, the idea of a universe filled with intelligent life has become part of our collective consciousness, helped along by cultural icons such as *Flash Gordon, Star Trek*, and *Star Wars*. For scientists, however, one big obstacle challenged this assumption: there was no direct evidence that there were other planets outside our solar system.

That all changed on May 28, 1998, when astronomer Susan Tereby of the Extrasolar Research Institute in Pasadena, California, announced the discovery of a planet around a double star just north of the constellation Taurus, about 450 light-years from Earth. The discovery was immediately hailed "as a landmark in our quest to understand our origins" by fellow astronomer Steve Strom of the University of Massachusetts. Anne Kinney of the Space Telescope Science Institute in Baltimore told the *Los Angeles Times* that the finding was potentially a "watershed event."

Tereby captured the image of the planet using the Hubble Space Telescope. Even with its enormous power of magnification, the discovery was something of a quirk. The enormous planet—about three times the size of Jupiter—was caught on film in that cosmic moment when it was actually being ejected from its solar system by some unknown cause. Astronomers have long suspected the existence of planets outside our solar system but could not see them because the stars' bright light drowned out their images. Tereby's wayward planet was far enough away from its binary sun to avoid the glare.

There was something else unusual about the planet: a 130 billion–mile–long glowing stream bridged the space between the binary stars and the planet, like a giant neon arrow pointing to it. For Charles Beichman, project scientist for NASA's Origins Program, "this tail of luminosity" convinced him that Tereby's discovery was more than pure speculation.

Still, as some astronomers have pointed out, what Tereby saw could have been a failed star called a brown dwarf, which are relatively common. Or perhaps it was an optical illusion—a background star that appeared to be something else on the Hubble image. Tereby recognizes that possibility but calculates the chance to be one in fifty.

Kinney defended the discovery, saying, "If is looks like a duck and it quacks like a duck, it's probably a duck." Tereby's planet, she said, raised the possibility that thousands of homeless planets are wandering about in our galaxy.

Wendy Friedman
MEANS FOR MEASURING THE UNIVERSE'S AGE

One of the most intriguing questions in astronomy is the age of the universe. Sixty years ago Edwin Hubble, the renowned astronomer after whom the space telescope is named, came up with an age that remained the benchmark until someone pointed out that it was less than half the age of the oldest rock on the surface of the earth.

The revised thinking placed the universe's age between 10 and 20 billion years. Despite the comfort zone in that range, astronomer Wendy Friedman challenged the accepted orthodoxy in 1994 by estimating the universe to be much younger, more like 8 to 12 billion years old. Her proof was in the pudding she invented: the first reliable means for measuring distance between heavenly bodies.

On November 26, 1994, Friedman announced to a packed press conference, "We have determined the distance to M-100 [a nearby galaxy] more accurately than has ever been done before. We find a distance to M-100 of 56 million light-years." She also announced that M-100 was moving away from Earth at a speed of 3 million miles an hour. With those speed and distance calculations in hand, it was easy to estimate—or reestimate—the universe's probable age.

Before Friedman's method, astronomers could measure the speed that faraway galaxies were moving away from us, but not the actual distance. It was like a light on a train pulling away somewhere in the background: was the light relatively close but faint, or was it bright but far away? Friedman showed how to determine distance in space, the other half of the equation in estimating the universe's age.

As is often the case in science, an answer leads to many more questions. Just as Hubble's original estimate of the universe's age didn't add up with the age of Earth's rocks, Friedman's estimate makes the universe younger than its oldest stars. There is enough margin in Friedman's calculations that the universe could be more like 15 billion years old, which would put it right on the mark with the oldest stars. More observations are being conducted with the Hubble Space Telescope to reduce this uncertainty.

However, if Friedman's original calculations are correct, then there's a new cosmic conundrum that calls into question the mother of all current orthodoxy, the Big Bang theory. Details at eleven.

And Let's Not Forget . . .

At twenty-six, **Kari A. Lewis** became the chief mission engineer for NASA's Deep Space 2 probes, a $29.2 million project designed to study the planet Mars's soil and atmosphere and to look for water. The two grapefruit-size "nanorovers" were successfully launched in 1999; however, contact with the probes was lost upon entry into Mars's atmosphere. Currently Lewis is the systems engineer for the MUSES-CN Nanorover mission, a collaboration between the Japanese Institute of Space and Astronautical Science and NASA. The aim of the mission, which is scheduled to launch in July 2002, is to take pictures and collect science data on the asteroid known as 1989 ML. . . . **Evelyn Boyd Granville** developed computer programs that were used for trajectory analyses in the Mercury Project (first U.S. manned mission in space) and in the Apollo Project (which sent astronauts to the moon). She also holds the distinction of being one of the first two African American women to earn a Ph.D. in mathematics, graduating from Yale in 1949. . . . **Aglaonike** of ancient Greece was known as a powerful sorceress who could make the sun and moon disappear at will, according to historical records. More likely she mastered the method for predicting lunar and solar eclipses. . . . The space immediately surrounding Earth is cluttered with man-made debris and naturally occurring meteoroids. Because objects in space travel at tremendous speeds, a tiny fragment can rip a hole in a pressurized spacecraft, resulting in an explosion. NASA research engineer **Jeanne Crews** and her team invented the Hypervelocity Impact Shield, which utilizes multiple layers of material with space in between that renders debris harmless by superheating and liquefying it. For astronauts it's the difference between having an insect splatting against the windshield and a bullet going through it. . . . Entrepreneur and engineer **Beatrice Hicks** pioneered the study and analysis of pressure and density devices used in aircraft and missiles. She was also the first president of the Society of Women Engineers. . . . **Margaret Grimaldi,** an aerospace engineer at the Lyndon B. Johnson Space Center in Houston, Texas, is the co-inventor of devices for spacecraft, including an escape system and a robot arm for building on a space station. However, it's her "memory alloy," which she developed with fellow NASA engineer **Leslie Hartz,** that promises widespread application. The metal can be reshaped many times and resume, under certain conditions, its original shape. This quality allows it to be programmed, for example, to turn a switch on and off at a certain temperature. . . . **Karen Castell,** an electrical engineer at the Goddard Space Flight Center, outside of Washington, D.C., was named on a NASA patent for her invention of the High Voltage Power Supply. Her device converts solar energy into high-voltage electricity needed to power specialized equipment, such as X-ray and gamma-ray detectors. She hopes to apply some of the technology to a Tropical Rainforest Measurement Project. . . . **Hatice Cullingford** invented three high-tech systems that were patented by NASA while working as a senior engineer at the Mars Exploration Office in Houston. Among these is the Apparatus for Next Generation Life Support Systems, which creates an artificial ecology through the recycling of air, water, food, and waste. Another of her inventions decreases the need for landfills on Earth by processing garbage (plant leaves, paper, etc.) right at its source. One happy by-product of the process is a clean-burning fuel. . . . **Bonnie Dunbar** earned a master's degree in ceramic engineering and, as a research engineer at Rockwell International, helped to develop the ceramic tiles that enable the space shuttles to survive reentry. In 1985 she had an opportunity to test those tiles firsthand, as an astronaut aboard the space shuttle *Challenger.* She would go on to participate in four more space flights, logging a total of fifty days in space. . . . **Dr. Rita Bernabei** of the Gran Sasso

National Laboratory in Rome led the team of scientists that presented the first evidence of the long-sought "dark matter," which astronomers believe makes up 80 percent of all mass in the universe. Many scientists believe that the substance, also known as a neutralino or WIMP (weakly interacting massive particle), is the first step toward an ultimate theory that would account for all known forces and particle behaviors in nature.

CHAPTER 8

Fun and Games

M aybe it all started during the Revolutionary War, when tavernkeeper Betsy Flanagan stuck a feather stolen from a local landlord's rooster into her signature drink, cried "Vive le coq's tail!" and invented the cocktail. Or maybe it was when poet/artist Rose O'Neill became millionaire/bohemian Rose O'Neill by designing the Kewpie doll. We're pretty sure it wasn't the day Dr. Katherine Perlman synthesized cannabis. But the fact is, women inventors have never been dull. They've had fun, and they've created fun. And sometimes they've made serious money doing it.

Ruth Handler
BARBIE DOLL

"For baby boomers," writes pop historian M. G. Lord in the book *Forever Barbie: The Unauthorized Biography of a Living Doll,* "Barbie has the same iconic resonance as many female saints. She is the archetypal female figure, something upon which little girls project their idealized selves." Fact: the average American girl owns eight Barbie dolls. Fact: Barbie is sold in 114 countries. Fact: Barbie and her line of accessories grossed $3.2 billion—that's billion with a B—in 1994 for toymaker Mattel.

Yet when Ruth Handler brought Barbie to the New York Toy Show in 1959, the powers that be said her doll was a dud.

Ruth Handler came up with the idea for Barbie by watching her young daughter, Barbara (nicknamed Barbie, of course), play with paper dolls. During the prefeminist days of the 1950s, it was assumed that little girls all fantasized about becoming mommies, so the toy industry provided them with baby dolls. But Handler knew that little girls also fantasized about being *big* girls and that her own daughter preferred "grown-up dolls with fashionable outfits," as she put it.

At the time Ruth's husband, Elliot, and his partner Harold "Matt" Matson were having some success with their toy company, Mattel (for "Matt" and "El-iot"). Ruth had helped them start the business by marketing their picture frames; soon the trio branched out into dollhouse furniture and toy musical instruments. Ruth went to the company's designers with her brainstorm.

"When I told my people what I wanted to do, they looked at me like I was asking the impossible," remembers Ruth. What she said was "We should make a doll like those paper dolls, but three-dimensional.

Ruth Handler parlayed a good idea into a Billion Dollar Doll. (Courtesy of Ruth Handler)

A doll with breasts and a narrow waist and painted fingernails." A living doll every little girl would want to grow up to be.

Eventually Mattel's engineers and technicians took her direction and created Barbie. (It is the engineers and technicians, in fact—not Ruth—who hold the patents.) A fashion designer was hired to create Barbie's wardrobe.

"The important thing about design is to know what you want, what the characteristics of the final product should be," explains Ruth Handler. "Then you get technicians to make it happen."

Despite the misgivings of the toy mavens at the New York Toy Show, Barbie happened in a big way. Within their first ten years, Barbie and Ken (named for Ruth's son, of course) earned $500 million. Ruth Handler did pretty well, too. By 1964 she and Elliot controlled Mattel stock worth $44 million, according to the *Wall Street Journal*. Ruth Handler became executive vice president, then president, then cochairman of the board of Mattel. These titles were unheard of for a woman in the 1960s. (Remember, women were still excluded from juries in 1963.)

Once, recalls Handler, she was the keynote speaker for an investment seminar and had to be smuggled into the meeting room, as it was held in a men-only club! In time she became a director of the Federal Reserve, a member of the National Business Council for Consumer Affairs, and a guest professor at prestigious universities like USC and UCLA.

But life was not always easy for the onetime secretary from Denver, Colorado. In 1970 she was diagnosed with breast cancer and lost first one and later both breasts to radical mastectomy. Despondent and assailed by business setbacks that included federal banking charges, Ruth and Elliot resigned from Mattel in 1978. Ruth Handler was down—but she wasn't out. She went to Peyton Massey, one of Barbie's original designers, and had him sculpt the Nearly Me breast prosthesis, so that other women could be spared some of the discomfort and embarrassment Ruth herself endured.

"I said, 'I want to make commercial breasts available to everybody, with separate rights and lefts that contour to the body, and in bra sizes.' He said I was crazy, but I convinced him to help me."

Handler's little Ruthton Corporation, which manufactured the Nearly Me, became a success in its own right. She sold it in 1991 to a subsidiary of paper giant Kimberly-Clark. "It's hard to retire," said Handler in 1992, sighing. "I've led a very, very busy life."

In her life as an inventor, Ruth Handler's modus operandi has always been simple: "I observed the need. I observed the void in the marketplace. And then I defined the product that would fill it."

Gertrude Rogallo
HANG GLIDER

The gliding part of a hang glider (as opposed to the hanging part) is known as the Rogallo Wing. It is not named for its inventor; it's named for its *inventors*, Francis and Gertrude Rogallo. While history has belittled Gertrude's contribution to the creation of the Rogallo Wing, Francis never did. He put her name on every patent, and he credited her as his partner and collaborator, even when the government wanted to call her his seamstress.

The first nonrigid, heavier-than-air flying machine, the Flexikite was created by the Rogallos as a plaything. It was the 1940s, and the Rogallos had three children whose kites kept breaking. Francis, an aeronautical engineer at Langley Field, wanted to design something as limp as a parachute that would swoop and dive like a kite. He and Gertrude made the first models from potato chip bags, then from nylon shrouds—finally the model that Gertrude sewed from some chintz kitchen curtains did the trick. The glazed fabric was less porous to the air and had a better lift.

To test their creation, Gertrude and Francis turned the front hall into a wind tunnel by setting up an electric fan in the kitchen. They fine-tuned the Rogallo Wing, patented it in 1948 as "a completely new concept" in flying machines, and sold it as a toy. Creative Playthings started manufacturing Flexikites in bright silvery Mylar, and they were an instant hit.

It didn't take the government long to notice that the Rogallo Wing was also a great way to float a space capsule back to Earth. NASA quickly coopted it, and the Rogallos patented many high-tech improvements to the design. They assigned all of them to the space program, gratis.

In 1968 NASA did award the Rogallos a generous cash bonus for their work. And in 1988 they commemorated the fortieth anniversary of the couple's invention by presenting Dr. Francis Rogallo an inscribed plaque. His co-inventor, Gertrude, was given . . . an attractive sewing kit.

But Gertrude Rogallo's work is neither denigrated nor forgotten by one large and avid group: hang-gliding enthusiasts. In 1993 the Rogallo Foundation was formed to "support education and research in aerodynamics and low speed aerodynamics, and promote outdoor recreational flying opportunities." And in all of the Rogallo Foundation literature, Francis and Gertrude Rogallo are pictured standing side by side as equal partners, just as they were in life.

Pamela Ryan
GIRL'S SOFTBALL HELMET

Pamela Ryan's daughters liked to play softball, but the lump created by their bunched-up ponytails made their helmets (1) uncomfortable and (2) fall off. This—and the fact that more than 7 million American girls play in softball leagues—inspired the Minnesota lobbyist and entrepreneur to design a softball helmet with an arch-shaped opening in the back, through which one can thread a ponytail.

In 1996 Ryan's helmet was licensed and distributed by the same company that makes the National Football League's helmets. Ryan stressed that boys who wear ponytails are also welcome to use the helmets—although boys may be less enthusiastic about her line of baseball caps. Each of Ryan's caps is embroidered with a quote from a prominent woman (e.g., "I'm not lucky. I deserved it."—Margaret Thatcher. Or "Don't compromise yourself. You're all you've got."—Janis Joplin), and a portion of the proceeds is donated to women's causes.

Mary Putre
"REVENGE" TOILET PAPER AND NOVELITY GIFTS

In the late 1980s Mary Putre was working the midnight shift as a data entry clerk—and she was miserable. She knew she had the talent to be an innovator, an entrepreneur; she knew she had good ideas. But how to begin?

"I would read about people who started out of garages, with little or no money," she says. But to take that step, to actually quit her job . . . it was too much to contemplate.

Fate took over in 1989. Putre got laid off.

"I got some severance pay," she recalls, "and on July eleventh, 1989, Eyecatcher gifts was born."

Her most successful product is Revenge toilet paper: "the only toilet paper that won't rip or tear." It is carried in five major gift catalogs. For this and her six other gift inventions, Putre employs sales reps all over the country.

"Getting laid off isn't always a bad thing," she says. "It can be a chance to make your dreams come true."

Dona Bailey
CENTIPEDE

Remember Pac-Man, and Space Invaders, and all those other arcade games that ate adolescent boys' quarters throughout the 1980s? Then you probably remember the first arcade game that caught on with female players: Centipede. Maybe it was the first successful crossover because it was the first coin-operated computer game designed by a woman. Her name is Dona Bailey.

Bailey, a former programmer for General Motors, joined the Atari Corporation in 1980; Centipede was her first assignment. It was her brief to make the game accessible to women and girls, to give it more personality than the point-and-shoot "twitch" games then dominating the market. Despite her success, Bailey was not happy in the world of game design. Calling it a "fraternity," Bailey left the male-dominated Atari in 1984 to work in other areas of the growing computer industry.

And Let's Not Forget . . .

Gertrude Ederle is best remembered as the first woman to swim the English Channel. But in 1933, she also patented a combination paddle and float for use by her fellow swimmers. . . . Responding to bluestocking legislation that made it illegal to change clothes on the beach, **Barbara Arnold** created the Change-A-Robe, a garment roomy enough so that you can discreetly slip on your bathing suit underneath it. Change-A-Robes became indispensable equipment on the set of the popular television series *Baywatch*. . . . **Julie Austin** couldn't find a water bottle in stores small enough and light enough that she could strap it to her wrist while running. So she made one herself. . . . Another runner, **Nancy Linday,** combined the best of the sun visor and the best of the baseball cap into the convertible Vicap. . . . Two Virginia couples, **Ann and Bill Schlotter** and **Ann and Tom Coleman,** designed a battery-powered lollipop. The Spin Pop rotates in your mouth to facilitate easy licking; amazingly, more than 15 million of the novelty item have sold. Both Anns have quit their day jobs at the post office. . . . The prototype of today's popular Monopoly board game was called the Landlord's Game and was created by one **Lizzie Magie** in the late 1800s. Another version was patented in 1924 by **Elizabeth Phillips.** Phillips sold her rights to Parker Brothers; they buried it in favor of a similar game patented by Charles Darrow, and the rest is his story. . . . **Elizabeth Kingsley** is credited with inventing the Double-Crostic puzzle. . . . The popular board game Balderdash was created by Canadian actress **Laura Robinson** and her buddy, copywriter Paul Toyne. They licensed the game to a manufacturer and have collected royalties on more than 5 million units sold worldwide. . . . Back in 1892 **Mary Slocum** patented an important improvement to the bicycle or, as she called it at the time, the velocipede. It was an integrated brake. . . . And modern cyclists, take note: **Laura Marion** holds Patent #5,020,852 for the Comfort Plus Bicycle Seat, the mother of all bicycle seats. It's softer, it's wider—it is, as Marion says, "firm but forgiving." . . . The first commercially viable disposable 3-D camera, marketed under the brand name Wowzer, was patented by **Maureen Meredith Day** as the Anagraphie Dimensional System. Wowzer is easier to remember.

They Can't All Be Winners . . .

In *Mothers of Invention* it was noted that "the best intentions of Sarah Ruth, Deniece Lemiere and Bertha Dlugi notwithstanding, if God had wanted horses to have sun shades, dogs to have spectacles, and parakeets to have diapers, She would have designed them Herself."

Happily, women are every bit as flawed today as they were then. Wouldn't it be boring if everyone were perfect?

Here are a few doozies from the innovative fringe:

Because "civilized women often do not have the opportunity to develop the muscles needed in confinement," **George and Charolette Blonsky** painstakingly assembled the Centrifugal Force Birther (Patent #3,216,423). The Birther is essentially a large wheel to which you strap a woman in labor and spin her around. This "loosens" the baby and "propels" it down the birth canal. Although patented back in 1965, the Birther has not yet been widely adopted by the obstetrical community. . . . Also ignored by the ob/gyns of the world is **Darlene Miller**'s Patent #5,235,974, a heated bra for lactating mothers. Wired to an electrical source and radiating heat around the breast, the Heated Bra Arrangement is supposed to "relieve engorged, lactating" women. If nothing else, it's a good source of relaxing warm milk. . . . No pregnancy is involved in **Rita DellaVecchia**'s 1989 invention, the Automatic Pet Petter. As billed, the device is a fake hand on a stick that when activated by an electric eye tirelessly pats the nearest dog or cat. DellaVecchia was awarded Patent #4,872,422 for her breakthrough. . . . **Reva Harris Keston** invented a receptacle in which to save used gum—forgetting the old song that warns about chewing gum losing its flavor on the bedpost (or in a box) overnight. . . . **Janet Dean** received Patent #5,008,964 for the Singing Potty, which presumably whistles while you work. . . . And in 1930 **Helene Shelby** received a patent for her Guilt Inducer for Criminals. She had, she claimed, a foolproof way to trick a suspect and "cause him, if guilty, to make a confession." The ruse? A skeleton with flashing lights for eyes, which would pop out from behind a curtain during interrogation. This would so frighten the weak-minded criminals that they would break down on the spot. Law enforcement has yet to embrace the concept.

CHAPTER 9

The Littlest Inventors

Children are great scientists. I'm afraid that as we grow up, our ability to question becomes suppressed. It's that ability to question everything that makes a scientist. And then, of course, to find the answer.

— Dr. Andrea Bodnar, inventor of synthesized telomerase

Kids have a different way of looking at things, and sometimes we come up with ideas others may not have thought of. I think we're willing to do a lot of things because we do them for fun, and we're not afraid to fail.

— Jamie Lynn Villella, age eleven, inventor

In the years since *Mothers of Invention* was published, both industry and academia have come to agree with Andrea Bodnar and Jamie Villella. Contests, clubs, and conventions for young aspiring inventors have sprung up all over. There's even a summer camp called Camp Invention.

The Duracell/NSTA Scholarship Competition is open to grades nine through twelve, and awards prizes worth up to $20,000. (Your invention must be battery powered, of course. . . .) Invent America! sponsors state, regional, and national competitions for student inventors. The Inventors Workshop International Education Foundation holds a "Great Idea Contest" for all ages. And the National Inventive Thinking Association provides speakers on the subject for schools around the country. Many states and even cities have their own organizations to promote inventive thinking by young people (see Appendix B).

There is no minimum age for innovation and creativity, any more than there is a gender requirement.

Jeanie Low
KIDDIE STOOL

Elizabeth Low
HAPPY HANDS

In March 1992 Texan Jeanie Low, then eleven years old, became one of the youngest women ever to be granted a U.S. patent when she was awarded Patent #5,094,515 for her Kiddie Stool. She had actually thought up the idea when she was still in kindergarten.

The Kiddie Stool is a clever concept, a fold-out stepstool that tucks under the bathroom cabinet so that your father won't trip over it and smash it to pieces the way he did with the old plastic one.

Jeanie Low soon saw her achievement overshadowed, however. In March 1994 she was superseded by a female inventor who was only ten when she got her patent. The upstart? Jeanie's younger sister, Elizabeth, who patented a novelty paperweight called Happy Hands.

By the time they were in their teens, the two girls became owners and operators of J&E Innovations. Between them they have invented everything from an alarm that sounds when the bathtub starts overflowing (Dad again) to prescription lenses for medical instruments.

Obviously problem solving runs in the family.

"I invented the Kiddie Stool because my dad would always break the plastic stepstools in the bathroom," says Jeanie. Dad, a Houston pediatrician, had raised his daughters to explore and innovate. When Jeanie thought up her Kiddie Stool, Mom and Dad encouraged her to build a prototype and to enter it in her school's invention fair. She placed first. Later she entered the stool in a statewide invention fair in Houston and again won first prize. This led to meetings with the Texas Creative Society and the Houston Inventors Association. One of the members of the latter group was a patent attorney.

"The patent attorney told me not to be upset if my patent didn't come through, but believe it or not, my patent came through on the first try," says Jeanie. "I am the only person in the world to have a folding stool like this."

Jeanie began to manufacture a prepackaged Kiddie Stool kit and has even had it displayed at the Smithsonian Institution in Washington, D.C.

"When they invited me," says Jeanie, "they didn't realize I was a kid. All they knew was I had a patent and my invention was good. I was the only kid there, and over ten thousand people came to see my invention."

Elizabeth Low also credits her father for inspiring her invention, but not because of his clumsiness. Rather, it was his profession that led to Happy Hands.

"Several afternoons a week after preschool I would go to my dad's medical office to visit. I found that the rubber gloves he wears when he examines patients are very elastic and that I could form them into lots of interesting shapes if I filled them with sand."

Soon Dr. Low was wondering where all his latex gloves were disappearing to: Elizabeth was taking them home, filling them with sand, and painting them in bright colors, turning them into animals and flowers.

Only four years old, Elizabeth was too young for any of the grade categories at the Houston Invention Society Exhibit at the local mall, so the organizers put her in with the kindergartners. Then they watched in amazement as judges awarded Happy Hands first place over the high school students' work.

"Almost everyone who sees Happy Hands wants one," says Elizabeth. Her next task was improving the pliability, durability, and salability of her Happy Hands. She says she must have tested one hundred varieties of rubber gloves, as well as innumerable combinations of sand and paint. The perfect mix—plus a well-timed "two for one" sale—led to a product good enough to sell to a very famous hand

indeed: Christopher Hart, the Hollywood actor who plays the disem-
bodied Thing in the *Addams Family* movies.

"I like to find solutions to problems in my life and other people's
lives," says Jeanie. Her latest invention is a gripping device that helps
people with arthritis—like her grandmother—open doorknobs more
easily. Jeanie has found a niche inventing items for the bathroom,
whereas Elizabeth specializes in the office.

"Concentrate on a particular inventing area, something you are
familiar with," advises the elder Low. "The invention must either ful-
fill a need, simplify a task, or fill a void. If there is not a good market
for the product, it will not succeed."

No wonder Jeanie and Elizabeth find themselves sought-after talk
show guests and classroom lecturers. How many adults have put it so
succinctly? One last piece of inventing advice from Jeanie Low, poised
to become a "Lady Edison" for the millennium:

"Don't reinvent the entire wheel; rather, modify a small part of it."

Abbey Fleck
MAKIN' BACON

"Good inventions are all about a problem that a lot of people have,"
says Abigail Mae "just call me Abbey" Fleck. "If you just go through
your daily routine and encounter a problem, think of a way to solve it.
That's how you make an invention that people would be interested
in."

It seems simple, but Abbey should know; she was a veteran inventor and entrepreneur before the age of ten. The young Minnesotan's
invention came to her at the breakfast table, watching her dad struggle
to drain the bacon. Today her idea is a top seller, and its royalties support the whole family.

The Makin' Bacon bacon cooker, a plastic stand that lets the grease
drip off the bacon while the bacon is browning, came to then-eight-
year-old Abbey one Saturday morning while her dad, a budding
inventor himself, was preparing breakfast. "He ran out of paper tow-
els, so he was laying the greasy bacon down on newspaper. And my
mom thought that was gross," recalls Abbey.

Dad held the bacon up in the air, joking, "We'll let it drip dry." And Abbey volunteered, "Why can't you just cook it hanging up?"

The observation seemed self-evident. Yet anyone who had been in a cookware department knew that there was no such thing as a hanging-bacon cooker on the market. The Flecks decided to build one.

"At first we used wooden dowels and a piece of Plexiglas. Then we tried part of a plastic hanger. It was a long process to find the right kind of plastic that wouldn't melt in the microwave," says Abbey.

In 1996 the Flecks patented their Makin' Bacon—in Abbey's name, since it was her idea—and consumers began ordering it from a coupon on the back of Armour brand bacon. Eventually the retail giant Wal-Mart began to stock the product; soon it became the top-selling item in the small housewares department.

"In some situations a younger person is a more natural inventor," says Abbey. "Older people are locked into a paradigm of how they do things. I think a lot of kids, if they were in the same situation as I was, probably would have said the same thing. It's just that their parents wouldn't have listened the same way."

Tracy Phillips
"Money Talks" Bill Reader for the Blind

Since 1982 the Duracell North Atlantic Group has been sponsoring an annual invention contest for junior high and high school students across America. Each year one hundred young inventors win prizes of up to $20,000 in savings bonds for creating "a working device that educates, entertains, makes life easier or performs some kind of practical function" and is battery powered.

The 1994 Duracell/NSTA Scholarship winner has gone on to see her invention awarded prizes at the International Science and Engineering Fair, the Westinghouse Science Talent Search, and the Academy of Applied Sciences.

Tracy Phillips was a junior at Long Beach High School in New York when Money Talks took first place at the Duracell contest. She was only seventeen and only the second female student to win the competition. But what is more extraordinary is the nature of her invention: so simple, so obvious, so inexpensive—and so necessary.

"It must be disturbing not to know if you are being cheated, simply because you cannot see the money someone hands you," says Phillips. "It must be demeaning to have to depend on the integrity and kindness of someone else for common money transactions. Wouldn't it be nice to give a blind person the independence to determine the value of a bill?"

All of this hit home to Tracy because her younger brother was born blind. Surely, she thought, if a soda machine can distinguish between a $1 bill and a blank piece of paper, and a stamp machine can tell the difference between a $5 bill and a $10 bill, there is some way to make a wallet that can do the same thing.

The theory is simple: as complex as the designs are on money, only a few certain key points distinguish one bill from the others. An inexpensive infrared light emitter and detector can "read" the "fingerprint" of the different bills, identifying it. The light energy is then converted to electrical energy and used to activate a voice chip. The entire device is powered by four AAA batteries and slips easily inside a wallet.

When the blind person places a bill into the Money Talks wallet, it tells you the denomination. Tracy is working on a similar electronic device that will read the content labels on foods and drugs to blind consumers.

Science, she says, should be creative, but it should also be compassionate.

K-K Gregory

WRISTIES

K-K Gregory is too young to serve on the board of directors of the company she founded. She is allowed to hold stock, however—which is a good thing, as the company is making money hand over, uh, wrist.

K-K was twelve in 1996, when she applied for patent and trademark protection on her Wristies, fleece hand protectors that keep the snow out of your sleeves. Almost before she had sewn up the first batch for her Bedford, Massachusetts, Girl Scout troop, McDonald's restaurants in Boston were ordering Wristies by the gross. They needed them to warm up their take-out-window employees in the harsh winter months.

Today the company sells Wristies by mail order and in sporting goods stores. Mom Susan Gregory runs the company on a day-to-day basis.

"It's really fun doing research on something and figuring out you're the first," says K-K, who thinks of herself as a designer first and a businesswoman second. Her ideal job? Designing Muppets characters for television.

Vanessa Hess
MAGIC SHINE COLORED CAR WAX

In 1991 Vanessa Hess was a twelve-year-old with a problem. Her science teacher had given her a challenging assignment: invent something within the next thirty days. Vanessa was sure that the only thing she was going to pull out of her hat was an F.

And then Vanessa helped her dad wax the family car. As they wiped off the wax, Vanessa noticed that the scratches in the paint were showing up white, where dried wax had gathered. It occurred to her that if the wax was the same color as the paint, it would make the scratches blend in instead of stand out.

Vanessa mixed paint pigment with car wax until she got a colored car wax that was good enough to enter in the Invent America! contest. She demonstrated her invention on a Matchbox toy car and went on to win first prize. When an auto-products company read about Vanessa in the newspaper, they contacted her and created a television infomercial for the new product, Magic Shine. Soon Vanessa was on television nationwide and her multicolored idea was raking in the green.

Becky Schroeder
GLO-SHEET

When *Mothers of Invention* was published in 1988, precocious inventors Jeanie and Elizabeth Low hadn't yet patented anything. They had barely begun to talk, for that matter. The youngest inventors on record at that time were sisters Teresa and Mary Thompson, who were eight and nine when they designed a solar tepee for the backyard. Betty Galloway was considered the youngest female to actually win a patent: she was ten years old when she was issued Patent #3,395,481 for her bubblemaking toy.

But the most successful preteen inventor documented in that book was undoubtedly Becky Schroeder, who holds Patent #3,832,556 for the Glo-Sheet, an acrylic board that illuminates the paper on top of it. Schroeder, from Toledo, Ohio, had conceived of the Glo-Sheet when she was ten years old and patented it when she was twelve. Her invention ended up supporting her.

It all started late one evening when Becky was sitting in a parked car waiting for her mom to return from running errands. Becky had homework to do, and she thought, "Wouldn't it be neat if there was some way to write in the dark? Maybe there's a way to 'light up' writing paper."

With the encouragement of her father—who happened to be a patent attorney—Becky set out to research phosphorescent materials and determine if in fact there *was* a way to light up writing paper.

Indeed, it turned out that there were many different ways to do it. There were chemiluminescent and bioluminescent materials, some of them quite inexpensive, that when exposed briefly to sunlight or a strong bulb would continue to glow on their own for a quarter of an hour or more. Becky created Glo-Sheets in which the whole page lit up and Glo-Sheets in which only the horizontal guide lines lit up. Over the next few years she received ten more patents for refinements to the Glo-Sheet.

Schroeder grew up to be the owner and operator of B. J. Products, manufacturing and marketing Glo-Sheets to police departments, hospitals, the U.S. Navy, and even NASA. Once again a child's "what if" had led to an adult's wherewithal.

Lisa Stovall
CHILD LOCATOR

"It's kind of like Lojack for people," explains Lisa Stovall. Her simple yet obvious idea—a tiny transmitter children can wear, to pinpoint their location in case they're ever lost or kidnapped—won her grand prize honors in an invention and design contest and has brought her the attention of news crews from as far away as Germany.

But it started out as a very sad story.

Eleven-year-old Lisa, from the small town of Montalba, Texas, was devastated when a local girl was kidnapped and murdered. An aspiring zoologist, Lisa had just seen a documentary about wildlife conservation and was particularly impressed by the sensors that game wardens use to monitor their charges. She figured if you could track down a missing dog inside an alligator's stomach, surely you could track down a missing child.

Since Lisa was the kind of girl who'd been making robots out of cardboard boxes since she was a toddler, she went to work turning her idea into reality. Though only in fifth grade, she contacted the Texas Parks and Wildlife Department and asked about the transmitters they use on wildlife. They educated her about the tracking devices and even loaned her a sample. She took it from there.

"I used the one they use for fishes," explains Lisa. "I wanted it to be really little. If someone did abduct somebody, I wouldn't want them to be able to find it." Lisa didn't need to invent the sensor technology; it already existed. Her idea was to adapt it for a new use. Her innovation: putting the sensor on a hair bow, so that a little girl could wear it inconspicuously.

The device—officially named the Child Locator: Lisa's Gift to Amber, in honor of the kidnap victim who inspired it—had manufacturers lining up to market it when it was ready. "It might make money," says Lisa, "but mostly I just want it to help."

Sarita James
SPEECH-RECOGNITION PROGRAMS

Normally Sarita James's "neural network" speech-recognition programs for computers would put her in the "Computer Liberation" chapter. But because she was only eighteen years old when she won the Student Nobel Prize for her work, she instead becomes a standout entry in this collection of young innovators.

The Brooklyn-born daughter of two doctors, Sarita was playing piano at the age of four. Later the family moved to Indiana, and she managed to study Latin at Homestead High School in Fort Wayne (and American public schools in the early 1990s were not known for their Latin departments). Sarita and her brother Rajesh both went on to study at Harvard University.

But it was when she was still in high school that Sarita became interested in neural networks and how they relate to computer speech recognition. Since there were no classes in neural networks at the high school level, she enrolled in college—while she was still a full-time high school student—so that she could continue her studies.

In simple terms a neural network is a relay of computer processors strung together to imitate the way the human brain thinks. One of the things computers had not been able to do until very recently was understand human speech. As Sarita explains, "Background noise, little or no pause between words, and many people talking at once distract the computer." To teach the computer to understand speech under the most difficult conditions, Sarita chose helicopters as a testing ground. Her invention, in fact, is technically known as Neural Network Phonetic Recognition of Helicopter Commands.

Using phonetic analysis—breaking words down into sounds, or phonemes—Sarita was able to make a computer understand human speech even in as noisy an environment as a helicopter. It was painstaking and repetitive work, but she persevered and broke through. Her accomplishment earned top prize at the 1994 International Science and Engineering Fair and a trip to Sweden to pick up her Student Nobel. She has been named one of the country's Top 20 Students by *USA Today* and profiled in *Time, Fortune, BusinessWeek,* and *Science News.*

Chelsea Lanmon
POCKET DIAPER

Had Chelsea Lanmon patented her handy Pocket Diaper when she invented it, she would win the "youngest inventor" title hands down. Because she was all of five years old when she designed the handy product, a kindergartner with two younger siblings and a precocious, problem-solving mind-set.

Like most kid inventors, Chelsea saw an everyday problem and addressed it head-on. "My little brother, Corbin, was a baby. Every time my mom changed him, I had to get the powder, wipes, and diaper," she says. "I wanted to find a way to get everything at once so I wouldn't have to be going back and forth."

In other words, laziness was the mother of invention.

Using little more than double-sided tape, Chelsea assembled a disposable diaper that packs its own powder and wipe. Simple. "I did a survey of mothers with babies, to find out if they would buy my Pocket Diaper," says Chelsea. "They wondered why nobody else had ever thought of that.

"People always wonder why they didn't think of a good invention first," muses Chelsea. "Most inventions are really simple, and anyone could think of them. But it is the most fun when you think of them first!"

Another of Chelsea's inventions is also really simple and extremely handy: the Super-De-Duper Ice Cream Scooper, a battery-operated ice cream scoop that heats up, to glide through the ice cream. She also invented a lightbulb-shaped attachment for irons called the Sleeve Smoother, to make it easier to iron the puffy sleeves on her dresses, and a smoke sensor for frying pans, to detect grease fires before they start.

Chelsea's inventiveness has already gotten her places she never expected to go: on television, to Washington, D.C.—and all before the age of ten. She says she expects to make inventing her life's work, and why not?

"Even though most of the time people think of boys as being the inventors, girls should remember that they can be inventors, too," says Chelsea. "Inventing is fun. Just try it!"

And Let's Not Forget . . .

Malibu in-line skater **Emily Hogan,** at age ten, invented the Safe&Sound noisemaking wrist guard ("the protective gear that speaks for itself") so that the big kids could hear her coming. . . . **Jana Kraschnewski,** the daughter of a chemist, perfected an environmentally sound plywood made out of cornstalk waste. She's trying to get manufacturers to help her mass-produce the product but is having trouble because she's still in junior high school. . . . In 1987 eleven-year-old **Hannah Cannon** invented alphabet playing cards and the game CARDZ. In 1990 she made history as the first child allowed onto the floor of the American International Toy Fair. . . . **Katie Harding** was only five in 1986, when she won the *My Weekly Reader* contest for combining an umbrella with a flashlight for those dark, wet mornings. . . . Twelve-year-old **Jennifer Garcia** combined a welcome mat and a vacuum cleaner to create the Vacuum Dirt Mat: it thoroughly cleans your dirty shoes before you walk into the house. Currently she's working on an Uncopy Machine, which will erase the ink on photocopies and allow the paper to be reused. . . . **Jamie Lynn Villella** has been inventing since she was in kindergarten. Her ideas include a shoe that grows with you, an improved thumbtack, a child-safe china cabinet, the "electronic neighborhood watch," and a new design for gardening tools that won the $200 first prize in a North Dakota invention convention. . . . **Hilde Anne Heremans** of Troy, Michigan, was seventeen when she invented a compass for the blind, which signals the different directions with musical tones. . . . **Wendy Jonnecheck** was in the fifth grade when she patented a new style of jump rope, which went on to be manufactured and distributed by Quality Industries of Hillside, Michigan. . . . Eight-year-old **Sarah Racine Cole** was so frustrated with burritos that fell apart when she tried to eat them that she devised Edible Food Tape, available in flavors like nacho cheese. . . . In 1987 **Suzy Goodin** was lauded by the World Intellectual Property Owners in Geneva for coming up with her Edible Pet Food Server at the tender age of six. Yet another youngster looking for a shortcut through chores, young Suzy wanted to avoid washing the yucky serving spoon after feeding the cats. She figured if she could scoop out their dinner with something the cats would actually eat, she could just drop it into their dish. She was right.

CHAPTER 10

Pathfinders and Forerunners

H ere's a quiz: Who said in the same breath, "Very few women are creative" and described Marie Curie, by any account among the greatest minds of the twentieth century, as having "the soul of a herring"? Well, it was one of the other greatest minds of the twentieth century, Albert Einstein. (He was having a debate with a woman physics student at the time.) A little professional jealousy? Perhaps. More likely Einstein was reflecting a cultural tunnel vision that women are intellectually inferior, and ergo, science and technology are beyond their grasp.

History would quickly make mincemeat of Einstein's, and society's, prejudice. The Atomic Age was ushered in on ideas that emanated from not only Marie Curie but an entire sisterhood of physicists. Curie's discovery and subsequent studies of radioactivity, for which she would win two Nobel Prizes (the first person ever to win two), laid the foundation. In the 1930s Ida Eva Tacke and Lise Meitner built upon Curie's work with their discovery of nuclear fission, the latter coining the term. Curie's daughter Irene, along with her scientific partner and husband, Jean-Frédéric Joliot, designed the first nuclear reactor, its construction halted on the eve of World War II.

Indeed, Einstein was virtually surrounded by distaff genius at the Manhattan Project, the covert program to build an atomic bomb in the United States during World War II. Among the most notable women were Maria Goeppert-Mayer, who would win a Nobel Prize for her theoretical analysis of atomic structure; Leona Marshall Libby, who directed the construction of the first thermal column; and Dr. Chien-Shiung Wu, who would be called "one of the giants of physics" upon her death in 1998 for her theory of the violation of atomic parity. Wu had commented on the irrational belief that men are better suited to science than women, saying, "I wonder whether the tiny atoms and nuclei, or the mathematical symbols, or the DNA molecules, have any preference for either masculine or feminine treatment."

It gets better. There's a good deal of circumstantial evidence that Einstein's work itself might have had assistance from a feminine mind. By all accounts his first wife, Mileva Maric, was a brilliant mathematician and physics student. They met in 1896 at the prestigious Swiss Federal Polytechnic Institute. Her admission there alone was a cause célèbre, as she was only the fifth woman ever to attend the school. She was certainly the only woman in Einstein's class. The story goes that Einstein met Maric when he asked her how she arrived at the solution to a particular mathematical problem—one, presumably, he had been unable to answer.

Their union produced two children but ended in bitter divorce. However, it was during the early years of their marriage that Einstein's most famous articles were published: on the theory of relativity, Brownian motion, and the photoelectric effect. Plenty of anecdotal evidence suggests that Maric continued to help Einstein solve his mathematical problems. At least one credible source, a member of the Soviet Academy of Sciences, said that the articles published in Russian originally listed Einstein and Maric as coauthors.

Of course, judging the dark side of Einstein's gender politics in the bright light of the late twentieth century may not be fair. At a time when women were still fighting for the right to vote, Einstein—and the rest of the world—looked but did not see the achievements of most women scientists and engineers. For by the early twentieth century, women had excelled not only in physics but in genetics, applied technologies, medicine, earth sciences, engineering, architecture, and agriculture. The fact is, innovations by women often laid the groundwork for the very inventions that made men famous.

The product of women's imagination was often quite concrete, tangible enough to be patented and, occasionally, even to be honored. But for all intents and purposes these inventors did not exist. "Women do not invent," said popular wisdom, and any inconvenient facts to the contrary somehow slipped between the cracks of history. These achievements would not be recognized by the news media nor, perhaps more important, included in textbooks. Call them the invisible inventors.

Here are but a few examples of the contributions to technology and science by "invisible inventors" who were Einstein's contemporaries:

- **The Reaper:** According to one historian, "The invention of the reaper was one of the most important events in the history of modern industry." The machine revolutionized the harvesting of hay and grain. In his patent, Cyrus McCormick cites the prior technology developed for the Manning Mowing Machine, invented in 1818, presumably by William Manning. Literature of the period, however, strongly suggests it was Manning's wife, Ann Harned Manning, who actually designed the Mowing Machine.

- **Skyscraper Construction:** nineteenth-century mathematician Sophia Germain developed the modern theory of elasticity, without which modern high-rise construction is inconceivable. Elasticity is the mathematical representation of stress and strain in materials such as steel girders. Her theory was put to the test in the erection of the Eiffel Tower; obviously it worked. When the builders inscribed on this wonder of the modern world the names of seventy-two people who made it possible, though, Germain was not among them.

- **Open-heart Surgery:** In 1935 Mary Hopkinson Gibbon, with her husband John Gibbon, invented a pump oxygenator that temporarily performed the function of the heart and lungs, thus making open-heart surgery possible.

- **Genetics:** In 1905 Nettie M. Stevens, Ph.D., published a monograph that identified the X and Y chromosomes and pinpointed their role in determining the sex of an embryo: the XX combination produces a female and the XY a male. Stevens's work outlined the future of modern genetics research, although one of her colleagues, Edmund B. Wilson, was credited with the discovery.

- **Children's Health Care:** Dr. Sara Josephine Baker established the field of child hygiene as a public health official in New York

City at the turn of the century. Her programs, which slashed the city's appallingly high infant mortality rates by four-fifths, would be adopted by all forty-eight states and many nations worldwide by the time of her retirement in 1923.

- **Electricity:** Twentieth-century British physicist Hertha Marks Aryton specialized in electricity and wrote what became a standard textbook, *The Electric Arc.* In 1904 she broke a gender barrier when she delivered a lecture before the most prestigious science organization of the day, the Royal Society in London. She also invented and patented a device for dividing a line into multiple lines.

- **The Brooklyn Bridge:** In 1873 Col. Washington Augustus Roebling was commissioned to build the Brooklyn Bridge, the first steel-cable suspension bridge. Unfortunately, Roebling became paralyzed, partly blind, deaf, and mute after a diving accident. His wife, Emily Warren Roebling, completed the bridge over the next decade, personally supervising all aspects of its construction from calculating stress analysis to reviewing structural requirements with representatives from steel mills. Her name appears nowhere on the official records of the bridge, but its builders dedicated it to her with an inscription on the East Tower.

Even the most visible women seemingly disappeared before the very eyes of male-dominated institutions when it came to their intellects. Film star and Einstein contemporary Hedy Lamarr, whose astonishing beauty earned her the sobriquet of "Hollywood's most beautiful woman," co-patented during World War II an advanced weaponry system that controlled torpedoes by radio. She had learned the basics of munitions when she was married in the 1930s to Austria's leading armaments manufacturer. Her idea proposed what is today known as frequency hopping, in which the receiver and transmitter change frequencies in sync, thus preventing signal jamming—the bane of radio communications.

When Lamarr approached the navy about her invention, it said she could better use her talents raising war bonds (which she did—$7 million worth in one night). When the patent ran out in the early sixties, engineers from the Sylvania Corporation redeveloped the system

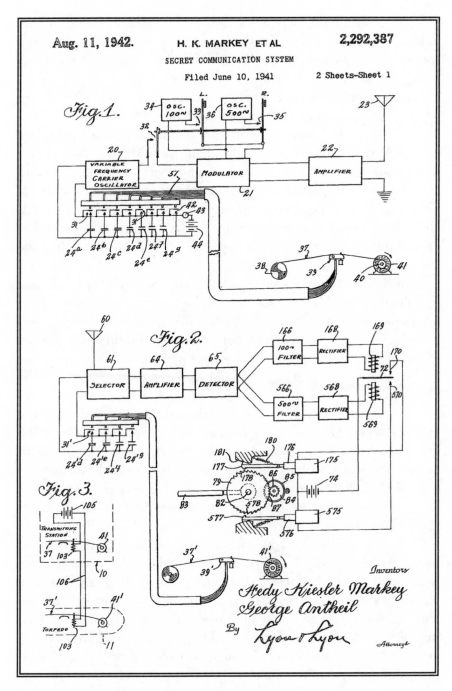

Aug. 11, 1942. H. K. MARKEY ET AL 2,292,387

SECRET COMMUNICATION SYSTEM

Filed June 10, 1941 2 Sheets—Sheet 1

Hedy Lamarr never wanted credit for the communications system she co-designed.

using state-of-the-art electronics, and it became a mainstay of U.S. military communications. Today it's widely recognized that Lamarr's concept of frequency changing is the basis for today's wireless technology, including cellular phones.

Not all men hold back women inventors, of course. There are plenty of instances in which fathers, husbands, and brothers assisted female innovators. Lamarr's co-inventor, avant-garde music composer George Antheil, thought her idea brilliant when she first approached him for assistance. Marie Curie's husband, Pierre, her soul mate and colleague, abandoned his own study of crystals to join her in her quest for radioactivity. (They shared the first of her two Nobel Prizes with A. Henri Becquerel.) Mars rover inventor Donna Shirley cites the influence and the encouragement of her father in her decision to become an engineer.

Indeed, too often women themselves were accomplices in their own invisibility. Betsy Metcalf, who qualifies as one of America's earliest inventors with her 1798 braiding machine, herself said that "many thought I ought to get a patent, but I told them I didn't wish to have my name sent to Congress." Antebellum plantation owner Catharine Littlefield Greene could have—should have—placed her name on the patent for Eli Whitney's cotton gin. Julia Hall worked beside her brother every day in their makeshift lab in the woodshed behind the Hall residence. However, only Charles's name appears on the 1886 patent for the method that made possible the cheap production of aluminum. Or take Amanda Theodosia Jones, who patented vacuum canning in 1872. Pressed on how a woman devised such a breakthrough invention, Jones credited her dead brother, who she said spoke to her in a series of dreams.

Denied access to the educational opportunities enjoyed by men, burdened by full responsibility for home and family, raised under a patriarchal culture and law (what's the point of filing a patent if it automatically becomes your husband's property?), women scientists and engineers were an oddity until recently. However, since 1950 the number of patents filed by women has increased fivefold. How will the entry of thousands of women change the fields of science and technology in the new millennium?

Einstein would eventually recant his opinion of Marie Curie, writing to her toward the end of her life, "I feel the need to tell you how much I have come to admire your spirit, your energy and your honesty. . . . I will always be grateful that we have among us people like you." But how much has society learned?

Nobel Prize–winner Christiane Nusselein-Volhard is considered the most important developmental biologist of the second half of this century. In 1975, while at the University of Basel—not too far in Switzerland from where Einstein and Maric met and studied—the brilliant postdoctoral student began to have doubts about her abilities. Her superiors viewed her work in embryology with indifference. At first she attributed it to her own inexperience or incompetence. "It took me a long time to realize that the issue was gender," she says. "They expected less of a woman. The attitude was 'I'll give her a chance, but I'm sure she won't perform.'" Fortunately Nusselein-Volhard decided not to just disappear—but what if she had?

In 1995, Marie Curie was entombed with honors in France's Pantheon, beneath an inscription that reads, ironically, "To the Great Men, a Grateful Nation." Then-president François Mitterand praised Curie for "the exemplary battle of one woman who decided to fight in a society dominated by men. . . . My hope is that equal rights for men and women will progress everywhere in the world because I find *undignified* [italics ours] in a civilized society the preference given to men for the last centuries." Well said, if not a little understated.

TIMELINE: A MORE COMPLETE CHRONOLOGY OF INVENTION

1616	Thermometer	Santorio Santorio
1648	Barometer	Blaise Pascal
1656	Pendulum clock	Christian Huygens
1668	Reflecting telescope	Isaac Newton
1679	Pressure cooker	Denis Papin
1711	Tuning fork	John Shore
1717	Smallpox variolation	Lady Mary Montagu
1755	Carbon dioxide	Joseph Black
1764	Spinning jenny	James Hargreaves
1784	Bifocal lenses	Benjamin Franklin
1793	Cotton gin	Catharine Littlefield Greene
1798	Smallpox vaccination	Edward Jenner
1804	Jacquard loom	Joseph Marie-Charles Jacquard
1806	Carbon paper	Ralph Wedgewood
1807	Steamboat	Robert Fulton
1819	Dental amalgam	Charles Bell
1821	Caffeine	Pierre-Joseph Pelletier
1823	Electromagnet	William Sturgeon
1826	Gas stove	James Sharp
1830	Lawn mower	Edwin Beard Budding
1831	Electric generator	Michael Faraday
1834	Reaping machine	Cyrus McCormick
1835	Six-shooter	Samuel Colt
1837	Braille	Louis Braille
1838	Morse code	Samuel Morse
1839	Vulcanization of rubber	Charles Goodyear

1846	Sewing machine	Elias Howe
1847	Chloroform	Jacob Bell and James Simpson
1848	SENECA FALLS CONVENTION BEGINS WOMEN'S RIGHTS MOVEMENT	
1852	Elevator	Elisha Otis
1855	Safety match	Johan Edvard Lundstrom
1860	Linoleum	Frederick Walton
1864	Pasteurization	Louis Pasteur
1867	Barbed wire	Lucien Smith
1868	Margarine	Hippolyte Megé-Mouries
1872	Vacuum canning	Amanda Theodosia Jones
1876	Phonograph	Thomas Edison
1877	Switchboard	Edwin T. Holmes
1878	Milking machine	L. O. Colvin
1879	Saccharin	Constantin Fahlberg and Ira Remsen
1880	Hearing aid	R. G. Rhodes
1883	Rayon	Louis de Chardonnet
1884	Fountain pen	Lewis Waterman
1885	Gas-engine automobile	Gottlieb Daimler and Karl Benz
1887	Contact lens	Eugene Frick
1891	Zipper	Whitcombe L. Judson
1894	Escalator	Jesse W. Reno
1900	Paper clip	Johann Vaaler
1900	WOMEN COMPETITORS INCLUDED IN OLYMPIC GAMES	
1901	Electric typewriter	Thaddeus Cahill
1901	Vacuum cleaner	H. Cecil Booth
1903	Windshield wiper	Mary Anderson
1906	AM radio	Reginald Fessenden

1908	Cellophane	Jacques E. Bradenberger
1909	Drip coffee	Melitta Bentz
1913	Stainless steel	Harry Brearley
1914	Brassiere	Mary Phelps "Caresse Crosby" Jacob
1915	JEANETTE RANKIN BECOMES FIRST WOMAN ELECTED TO CONGRESS	
1917	Sonar	Paul Langevin and Robert Boyle
1920	NINETEENTH AMENDMENT RATIFIED, GRANTING WOMEN'S SUFFRAGE	
1921	Lie detector	John Larsen
1922	REBECCA FELTON BECOMES FIRST WOMAN U.S. SENATOR	
1926	Aerosol can	Erik Rotheim
1927	Pop-up toaster	Charles Strite
1929	Electron microscope	Max Knoll and Ernst Ruska
1929	Frozen food	Clarence Birdseye
1931	Electric razor	Jacob Schick
1935	Invisible glass	Katherine Blodgett
1936	Helicopter	Henrich Foche
1938	Teflon	Roy Plunkett
1941	Dacron	John Whinfield
1944	Tupperware	Earl W. Tupper
1948	Electric guitar	Leo Fender
1948	Velcro	Georges de Mestral
1951	Disposable diaper	Marion Donovan
1952	Scotchgard	Patsy Sherman
1953	Automatic flight control	Irmgard Flugge-Lotz
1955	Polio vaccine (killed virus)	Jonas Salk
1956	FORTRAN	John Backus and team

1956	Correction fluid	Bette Nesmith Graham
1957	Polio vaccine (live virus)	Albert Sabin
1957	Immunosuppressants	Gertrude Elion and George Hitchings
1959	COBOL	Grace Murray Hopper and team
1960	FIRST COMMERCIALLY AVAILABLE BIRTH CONTROL PILL GOES ON SALE	
1964	Kevlar	Stephanie L. Kwolek
1964	TITLE VII BANS GENDER DISCRIMINATION IN EMPLOYMENT	
1965	BASIC	Thomas E. Kurtz and John G. Kemeny
1966	Signal generator	Betsy Ancker-Johnson
1967	Pulsars	Jocelyn Bell
1969	PASCAL	Niklaus Wirth
1972	Video game	Noland Bushnel
1973	CAT scan	Allan Macleod Cormack and Godfrey N. Hounsfield
1975	FIRST WOMAN ADMITTED TO U.S. MILITARY ACADEMY	
1976	Fabric softener	Annie S. Giordano
1981	SANDRA DAY O'CONNOR BECOMES FIRST WOMAN SUPREME COURT JUSTICE	
1982	Artificial heart	Robert Jarvik
1982	t-PA	Diane Pennica
1985	AZT	Janet Rideout and team
1986	Synthetic skin	G. Gregory Gallico III
1988	First patented animal life	Philip Leder and Timothy Stewart
1997	Cloning	Ian Wilmot
1998	WOMEN SURPASS MEN IN NUMBER OF COLLEGE DEGREES	

APPENDIX A:
JOINING THE RANKS...

So you, too, have a great idea and are poised to join the next generation of patenting females. Here's a primer on the patent process:

What Is a Patent?

There have been inventors and inventions long before there were patents. Prior to 1624, when the British Parliament established the modern-day patent system, inventors had little protection under the law. Anyone who wanted to could make, market, and profit from the innovations of another. In fact, bestowing exclusive rights to "any new manner of manufacture" was a common form of royal favoritism.

Tired of seeing only the king's cronies benefit from the latest advances, Parliament declared that patents would hereby be awarded to the actual inventor. Aside from being fair and ethical, this provided a powerful financial incentive for technological change.

Those upstarts in America wrote the right to patent into the U.S. Constitution, Article I, Section 8:

"The Congress shall have the power . . . to promote the Progress of Science and Useful Arts, by securing for limited Times to Authors and Inventors the exclusive Right to their respective Writings and Discoveries."

A patent, essentially, is a federal document that gives you legal ownership of your invention. It becomes like any other form of property: it can be inherited, sold, rented, mortgaged, and taxed. At least, for its seventeen-year term of exclusivity.

More than 5 million patents have been filed in America since the first one went to Samuel Hopkins in 1790. The first patent granted to a woman, Hannah (Mrs. Samuel) Slater, came only three years later, in 1793, for a new method of making sewing thread.

What Can Be Patented?

Any product, process, apparatus, or composition may be patented, including living matter, like genetically engineered bacteria. Plant hybrids and ornamental improvements can also receive Plant patents or Design patents.

We usually think of a standard Utility patent as being granted for the traditional "better mousetrap": some kind of machine. In fact, up until 1880 you had to present the Patent and Trademark Office with a working model of your invention in order to have it patented. No longer. Today patents are granted for everything from genetically engineered soy beans to computer algorithms.

To be patentable, an invention must be "new, useful and nonobvious." An invention is new if it has not been shown in "the prior art": in other words, has not already been patented or described in printed material. "Useful" means, that it should probably work—although patents are sometimes granted to "prophetic" inventions whose proof comes along later. And it should be "not so obvious that a person of ordinary skill" could have made it herself.

Do I Need One?

If you think you can make a profit of more than, say, $5,000 from your invention (it costs money to patent!), you might want to patent it. Even if you don't plan to manufacture it yourself, you can license it and collect a royalty. However, most inventions never make a penny.

It's always a good idea to do a marketing survey before starting the patent process: if I manufacture this item, will people actually buy it? The catch-22 is that once you "disclose" your idea to anybody, you have only one year from that point to file for the patent.

Remember also that a U.S. patent protects only your rights in the United States. Just as your right to vote does not extend outside the country of which you are a citizen, patent rights are enforceable only in the jurisdiction for which you have received the patent.

How Do I Get One?

In simple terms, you pay a fee to the Patent and Trademark Office (PTO). If they determine that your patent is "new, useful and nonobvious," the patent is granted. You maintain the patent by paying more fees at 3 and a half, 7 and a half, and 11 and a half years.

But those are the *simple* terms. Deciding whether or not something is in fact "new" is a process that takes about two years and usually costs thousands of dollars in legal fees. Since the U.S. patent system awards exclusivity to the "first to invent" rather than the "first to patent" (as it is in some countries), you have to prove that you were the first person who thought up the idea. Easier said than done.

Here are some steps you can take to protect your invention:

1. Keep an inventor's diary. Describe your invention in detail, and maintain a log of experiments and improvements. Sign and date each page. Have a trusted friend review each page and sign and date them as well, with the words "read and understood by . . ."

2. Explore the marketplace. Look in stores for similar products. Compare your product to what is currently available in terms of novelty, utility, and price. Determine what it would cost to manufacture your product. Remember that if you disclose your invention during this process, the clock is ticking: you have one year to file for your patent.

3. File for a patent. This currently costs about $400. The Patent and Trademark Office will examine the application, which takes six to nine months, and issue what is called an Office Action. Typically the first Office Action rejects some or all of the patent claims. It normally takes at least two exchanges between the inventor and the patent examiner to resolve all the issues, which is why many people choose to take the next step.

4. Consult a patent attorney. Patent attorneys charge from $1,500 to $5,000 for their expertise. There are also patent agents who will help you do a basic patent search for about $350, and also some attorneys who will review the do-it-yourselfer's paperwork for about $1,000.

5. Currently it takes eighteen to twenty-two months from filing to complete the patent process. During that time the application is kept secret and the inventor has the right to put "Patent

Pending" on the product. While this provides no legal protection, it does put potential poachers on notice.

Two new programs of the Patent and Trademark Office offer interim protection for the budding inventor. One is the Disclosure Document Program, a service provided by the PTO. This will accept and preserve for two years a paper describing the invention, helping the inventor prove when she first conceived the idea. (The Disclosure Document is not a patent application, and the date of receipt will not become the effective filing date of your later application.)

To participate in the Disclosure Document Program, send two copies of a signed description of your invention and a drawing. Include a self-addressed, stamped envelope and $10. You will receive one set of your papers back as proof.

Slightly more formal is the Provisional Patent Application. This is an inexpensive (currently $75) way of proving your invention is patent pending. It is not a patent application, though, and you still have one year to file for a patent.

To participate in the Provisional Patent program, submit to the Patent and Trademark office essentially the same description and drawings you plan to submit later for the actual patent.

More questions? The folks at the Patent and Trademark Office have lots of printed information to share. Contact them at: U.S. Patent and Trademark Office, 2121 Crystal Drive, Arlington, VA 22202,(800) PTO-9199, www.uspto.gov.

Also, see Appendix B for a terrific assortment of Web sites that can offer unlimited assistance to inventors. Thanks to the Internet, it's even possible to do your own patent search and learn about patent laws of other nations.

So get to it. And . . . good luck!

APPENDIX B:
RESOURCES

When I can no longer create anything, I'll be done for.

—Coco Chanel, fashion innovator

Want to learn more about women inventors, scientists, and discoverers? Need help in bringing the product of your imagination to market? There is a wealth of information available online through the Internet and through various organizations and institutions. Consider these resources:

Contemporary Women's Issues: This database contains over twelve hundred reports and periodicals covering issues of interest to women, including science and technology. It's especially good at summarizing the lastest lectures and symposia about women inventors. A recent edition, for example, summarized a conference on women inventors in Asia. It also links to organizations in various countries that promote and assist women inventors. The easiest way to acces the CWI database is through Electric Library via the Internet at www.elibrary.com and then search for "women inventors."

Intellectual Property Owners: IPO is a nonprofit organization representing people who own patents, trademarks, copyrights, and trade secrets. It sponsors the Spirit of American Ingenuity Award and the National Inventor of the Year Award. Members receive a semimonthly *Washington Brief* and a quarterly newsletter. For more information call (202) 466-2396.

Invent America!–U.S. Patent Model Foundation: In addition to providing educational materials, this organization sponsors the Invent America! contest for elementary and middle school students in the U.S. For more information call (703) 684-1836.

InventNET–The Inventors Network: A Web site and membership organization, the online aspect provides resources on inventor trade shows; directories for patent attorneys, agents, and U.S. and international inventor organizations; and a digest of patent news. Visit the site at www.inventnet.com.

Inventure Place–National Inventors Hall of Fame: Dedicated to inspiring invention in people of all ages and educational levels, this institution aims for nothing less than becoming a national center of innovation. It offers the Inventors Workshop, an educational outreach program, and sponsors the National Inventors Hall of Fame. For more information call (330) 762-4463.

Innovation Institute: This group, part of the Wal-Mart Innovation Network, provides inventors with an objective analysis of the risks and potential of their ideas. Its goal is to stimulate new job opportunities for Americans by cultivating ingenuity. For more information call (417) 863-0300.

Network of American Inventors and Entrepreneurs: A not-for-profit organization composed of inventors that gives practical tips on how to bring a product to market. Find them on the Internet at www.flash.net/~cgenius/naie.

PatentCafe.com: Devoted to intellectual property–including invention, business, tech, and law–this Web site features an international calendar of invention-related events, a digest of daily patent news, inventors' advice, and a digital registry for documenting your invention date (although this is not a substitute for filing a patent with the U.S. Patent Office).

U.S. Patent and Trademark Office: Have an idea but want to make sure someone hasn't already thought of it first? You can conduct your own patent search at no charge via the Patent Office's new Web site at http://patents.uspto.gov/.

Women Inventors Network: Established in 1995, this organization is composed mainly of women inventors' organizations or sections of women in inventors' associations in eight countries: Argentina, Canada, Cuba, Finland, Japan, Malaysia, the

Philippines, and Sweden. It publishes a semiannual newsletter and offers several reference books on invention, such as *International Invention Guide* and *Women Inventors Organizations*. Visit their Web site at www.invention-ifia.ch/ifiawin.htm.

Women Inventors Project: Based in Canada, this nonprofit organization provides a wealth of information on entrepreneurship for the woman inventor wherever she might live. Books, videos, and even games are available for purchase, designed to encourage women of all ages to pursue careers in technological innovation and scientific endeavors. For more information call (416) 243-0668 or visit their Web site at www.interlog.com~womenip.

www.WWWomen.com: One of the premier search directories for women online, this "supersite" has especially good science and technology areas with dozens of links to women's professional organizations, women's studies programs at colleges and universities internationally, and miscellaneous Web sites ranging from the esoteric ("Butterfly Lady, noted lecturer and educator of monarch butterflies") to the all-inclusive ("4,000 Years of Women in Science"). There's also a long list of sites that profile individual women inventors and scientists and a very good bibliography of printed reference materials.

INDEX

A

Abbott Laboratories, 95, 96
Activase, 107–109
acyclovir (Zovirax), 92
age of universe, measuring, 165–166
aging machine, 70–71
Aglaonike of Greece, 166
agriculture, 9–11, 115, 130, 191, 194
AIDS, 91, 93–94, 95–97, 101
Airbus, 35
aircart, 28–29
airline reservations system, 73
Alexander, Hattie, 90
Allen, Antonette C., 114
Altschul, Randice, 3, 32–33
Alvarez, Christopher P., 114
Ambrose, Valerie, 151
Amram, Fred, 2
Ancker-Johnson, Betsy, 59
Anderson, Mary (windshield wiper), 3, 19–20
Anderson, Mary (Women's Bureau), 6
Animal Safety Belt, 34
Antheil, George, 194
Apgar, Virginia, 91
Apparatus for Next Generation Life Support Systems, 167
Arnold, Barbara, 175
Aryton, Hertha Marks, 192
ASK, 83

Askins, Barbara S., 114
aspirin, "buffered," 113
astrolabe, 151
astronomy, 151, 163–166
atomic bomb, 84
Austin, Julie, 175
aviation, 151–152
AZT, 91, 93–94

B

Babbage, Charles, 67
baby jumper, 43
bacteriology, 21, 50
Bade, Maria, 113
Bag Bath, 113
Bailey, Dona, 174
Baker, Josephine, 147
Baker, Sara Josephine, 191–192
Baldwin, Anna, 34
Baranski, Celeste, 31–32
Barbie doll, 150, 169–171
Barry, David, 94
Bath, Patricia, 104–107
Beano, 56
béchamel sauce, 57
Beck, Angie, 150
Becker, Luann, 162
Bell, Jocelyn, 160
Benerito, Ruth, 58, 122
Benjamin, Harry, 80
Benjamin, Miriam, 34
Bentz, Melitta, 3, 39–40
Berezin, Evelyn, 59, 73

Bergh, Jean, 34–35
Berman, Bertha, 47
Bernabei, Rita, 167–168
Berson, Solomon, 100
Bianconi, Patricia A., 15–16
Bilas, Frances, 84
Billings, Patricia, 11–13
biochemistry field, 38, 119–121
Biosyn, 113–114
Bissel, Anna, 40–42
Bissett, Enid, 136
Blackwell, Elizabeth, 89, 91
Blanchard, Helen Augusta, 3, 53
Blanchard, Madame, 151–152
Blissymbols, 75–76
Blonsky, Charolette, 176
blood plasma substitute, 121
Bodnar, Andrea, 109–111, 177
"body work," 103–104
bone marrow transplants, 101–102
Boone, Sarah, 47, 57
Bottinick, Miriam, 34
Bourgeois, Louyse, 111
bra ("brassiere"), 134–140
Brazil, Rondônia province in, 119
bread, whole-wheat, 57
Brease Toilet, 58
breast prosthesis, 150, 171–172
Brinnand, Tana, 6
Brown, Rachel, 2, 97–99
Bryan, Lydia Aguilar, 113
Bryenton, Elizabeth, 130
Buchanan, Michelle, 35
buckyballs, 162
Budd, Isabelle, 150

building material, 11–13, 30, 127–128, 188
Burns, Red, 83
Burroughs-Wellcome, 92–93
Burson, Nancy, 70–71
Butterick, Eleanor, 38
Byron, Ada, Lady Lovelace, 59, 66–68

C

Cadolle, Herminie, 134–135
calculator, graphical, 77–78
Cannon, Hannah, 188
carpet sweeper, 40–42
Carson, Rachel, 116
car tray table, 30–31
Cartwright, Jessie, 57–58
Casey, Susan, 2, 43
Castell, Karen, 167
Catcher, Mikie B., 131
Centeno, Margarita, 127–128
Centipede arcade game, 174
ceramic tiles for space shuttle, 167
Change-A-Robe, 175
Chatham, Alice, 158–159
chat room guides, 83
Cheaper by the Dozen (movie), 54
chemistry
    artificial diamonds, 15–16
    Kevlar, 7–8
    kid-sensitive fingerprint kit, 35
    molecular filters, 128
    patents granted to women in, 89

Scotchgard, 46–47
chemotherapy, 91–93
child hygiene, 191–192
Child Locator, 184–185
Chilton, Annie, 34
chronology of invention,
    197–200
Clarke, Edith, 77–78
COBOL (Common Business
    Oriented Language), 62,
    86
Cochran, Jackie, 152
Cochran, Josephine, 3, 38–39
coffeemaker, drip, 39–40
Cole, Pamela, 131
Cole, Sarah Racine, 188
Coleman, Ann and Tom, 175
Collen, Désiré, 108
Computer Engineering
    Associates, 74
computers
    compiler for, 60–63
    ENIAC, 84–87
    gaming for, 63–66, 174
    microelectronics chip design,
        81–82
    network debugging system for,
        74–75
    prediction of, 67–68
    3-D innovations, 76–77
    voice-controlled devices,
        16–18
    See also software
computer science classes, 59–
    60
Conceiving Ada (film), 68, 69
condom, 150
Conway, Lynn, 59, 78–82

Cooper, Penny, 47
Cooper, Sarah, 56
Cori, Gerty, 89, 100
Corner, Ann-Marie, 113–114
Coston, Martha, 23–25
cotton gin, 9–11, 194
Covermark, 150
Crews, Jeanne, 167
Crick, Francis, 110
Crixivan, 95
Criz, Brenda S., 114
Cronin, Betty, 50
Crosby, Caresse, 3, 134,
    135–136
Cullingford, Hatice, 167
Curie, Marie, 189, 194–195
Curie, Pierre, 194

D
Dale, Virginia, 118–119
"dark matter," evidence of,
    167–168
Davenport, Emily Goss, 28
Davidson, Jan, 83
Davis, Nancy, 113
Day, Maureen Meredith, 175
Dazzle Dot Lipstick Mirror,
    143–144
Dean, Janet, 176
DellaVecchia, Rita, 176
Demorest, Ellen, 38
De Osorio, Ana, 89
Deubener, Lydia, 28
diamonds, artificial, 15–16
diaper, disposable, 149–150
diatom, 116
Dieceland Technologies, 33
Dieterich, Fred, 1

disabled persons, aids for, 16–18, 74, 83, 181–182, 188

Disclosure Document Program, 204

discoveries in space, 160–166

Discovery space shuttle, 157

dishwasher, automatic, 38–39

Dolman, Leslie, 83

Donovan, Marion, 3, 149–150

Double Breast Prosthesis, 150

Downing, Elizabeth, 77

Drucker, Doris, 29–30

dry cleaning, 58

Dunbar, Bonnie, 167

Duracell/NSTA Scholarship Competition, 177, 181

dynamic instruction scheduling (DIS), 80

E

Earhart, Amelia, 152

eco-software, 118–119

Ederle, Gertrude, 175

Edible Food Tape, 188

Edible Pet Food Server, 188

Edmark, Tomina, 141–142

Eglin, Ellen, 47

Einstein, Albert, 189, 190, 194–195

elasticity, theory of, 191

electricity, 192

elevated train, reducing noise of, 116

Elion, Gertrude, 2, 3, 90, 91–93, 102

ENIAC (Electronic Numerical Integrator and Computer), 84–87

Environmental CAT Scanning method, 129–130

EO, 31

Esalen Institute, 103

Esser-Mittag, Judith, 144–145

ethnomedicine, 124–126

Expandable Jock Strap, 133

extraterrestrial life discovery, origin of life, 160–161, 162

Eyecatcher gifts, 174

F

fabric softener sheets, 42–43

Face Software, 70, 71

facilitator cell, 101, 102

Fausto-Sterling, Ann, 2

fertilizer, 115, 130

Finley, Alexandra, 131

Flanagan, Betsy, 169

Flanigen, Edith M., 128

Fleck, Abbey, 180–181

Flick, Sandy, 30–31

flour, high-protein, 131

Flugge-Lotz, Irmgard, 152

food preservation, 20–21

Foster, Asa Devlin, 33–34

Fox, Sally, 117–118

FoxFibre, 117–118

Franklin, Rosalind, 95, 109

Free, Helen Murray, 2, 100

frequency hopping, 192

Friedman, Wendy, 165–166

Frozen Food Hall of Fame, 52

Fu, Caroline, 74

fuel alcohol, 128–129

fungal disease, 97

Future Computing, 72

G

Galloway, Betty, 184
games for computer, 63–66, 174
Garcia, Jennifer, 188
Garcin, Caroline, 53–54
Garis-Cochran Washing
    Machine Company, 39
gender identity, 79–80
Genentech, 107, 108
General Foods, 50–51
genetics, 191
Geobond, 11–13
Germain, Sophia, 191
Geron Corporation, 109, 110
Getty, Jeff, 101
Ghez, Andrea, 163
Gibbon, Mary Hopkinson, 191
Gibson Girl, 6
Gilbreth, Lillian Moller, 54–55
Gleason, Kate, 3, 25–26
Glo-Sheet, 183–184
Goeppert-Mayer, Maria,
    189–190
Goldstine, Adele, 86, 87
Goodin, Suzy, 188
Goodyear Aquatred tire, 34–35
Gould, Charles Henry, 13
Graham, Bette Nesmith, 13–15
Granville, Evelyn Boyd, 166
"grass widows," 14
Green Box, 131
Greene, Catharine Littlefield,
    9–11, 194
Gregory, K-K, 182–183
Grene, Ethel, 150
Grimaldi, Margaret, 167
Gross, Elizabeth, 130–131
Gurer, Denise, 60

H

hair relaxer, 145–147
Hall, Julia, 194
Hall, Rill, 58
handbag, recyclable, 127
Handler, Ruth, 150, 169–172
hang glider, 172–173
Happy Hands, 178, 179
Harding, Katie, 188
Harger, Hannah, 3, 38
Hartz, Leslie, 167
Hayes-Roth, Barbara, 83
Hayflick Limit, 110
Hazen, Elizabeth, 2, 97–99
Headbenz, 150
Heeter, Carrie, 83
herbal remedies, 124–126
Heremans, Hilde Anne, 188
Herschel, Caroline, 151
Hess, Vanessa, 183
Hewish, Anthony, 160
Hicks, Beatrice, 167
high definition volumetric
    display (HDVD), 76
high-tech home, 71–73
High Voltage Power Supply, 167
Hildegard, Abbess, 89
Hills, Mary Ellen, 143–144
Hitchings, George, 92
Hobby, Gladys, 90
Hobson, Mary, 38–39
Hogan, Emily, 187–188
Holloway, M. Katharine, 3, 93,
    95–96
Holsinger, Virginia, 55–56
home management, 54–55
Hoover, Edna Schneider, 59, 77,
    78

Hopper, Grace Murray, 3, 59, 60–63, 74–75, 86
Horse Detacher and Brake, 34
Hosmer, Harriet, 30
hospital design, 112
household goods, patents for, 37
Howe, Elias, 53
Howell, Elizabeth, 58
Howell, Mary, 28–29
Hubble Space Telescope, 164, 165, 166
Huhn, Susan, 34
Hunnicut, Jane, 150
Hypatia of Alexandria, 151
Hypervelocity Impact Shield, 167
Hyworon, Zoriana, 83

I
ice cream cone, 58
ice cream freezer, 57
Ildstad, Suzanne, 3, 101–102
Imuram, 92
Induco Coal Conditioner, 131
infomercials, 49
Inspire Pharmaceuticals, 94
Institute for Cellular Therapeutics, 101, 102
Intellihome, 71–73
internal programming, 86
Invent America!, 177–178, 183, 205
invention, protecting, 203–204
Inventors Guild of America, 23
Inventors Hall of Fame, 91, 97

Inventors Workshop International Education Foundation, 178
ironing board, 57
Irwin, Harriet, 37
Isaacson, Portia, 71–73
I.V. House, 113
IV fluids, 119–121

J
Jacob, Mary Phelps ("Polly"), 3, 134, 135–136, 137, 138
Jagger, Janine, 4, 113
James, Sarita, 185–186
Jeanes, Allene Rosalind, 119–121, 124
Jell-O, 56–57
Jennings, Jean, 84, 86
Jerom, Sarah, 1
Jogbra, 139–140
Johnson, Nancy, 57
Joliot, Irene, 189
Jolly Jumper, 43
Jones, Amanda Theodosia, 3, 20, 38, 194
Jones, Charlotte Foltz, 57
Jonnecheck, Wendy, 188
Joyner, Marjorie, 147–149

K
Katalavox, 17–18
Keichline, Anna W., 34
Kempf, Martine, 16–18
Kenner, Beatrice, 150
keratoprosthesis surgery, 107
Keston, Reva Harris, 176
Kevlar, 7–8
Kiddie Stool, 178–179
Kingsley, Elizabeth, 175

"King's Quest" computer game, 65–66

Kinney, Anne, 164, 165

Kleiman, Kathryn, 87

Klein, Chips, 150

Knight, Margaret, 26–28

Knox, Rose Markward, 56–57

Kraschnewski, Jana, 188

Kucik, Dorothy, 126–127

Kurtzig, Sandra, 83

Kwolek, Stephanie, 2, 3, 7–8

L

Lactaid, 55–56

Lamarr, Hedy, 3, 192–194

Lanmon, Chelsea, 186–187

Lap Top Commuter, 30–31

laser cataract surgery, 104–107

Latham, Carol, A., 82

Laurel, Brenda, 82

"La Veuve Clicquot" champagne, 115

lazy Susan, 58

Leeson, Lynn Hershman, 68–69

Lefebre, Mme, 115

LesStrang, Barbara, 150

Lewis, Kari A., 166

Libby, Leona Marshall, 190

library database, 74

Lichterman, Ruth, 84

Lindahl, Lisa, 139–140

Linday, Nancy, 175

Liquid Paper, 13–15

"living battery," 130–131

Low, Jeanie and Elizabeth, 178–180

Lu, Shin-Yee, 76–77

Luce, Therese, 34

Luna, Bernadette, 158, 159

Luria, Susan, 34

lymphatic system, 112

M

Macdonald, Anne L., 2

MacDonald, Elizabeth, 52

MacGill, Elsie, 152

Magic Shine colored car wax, 183

Magie, Lizzie, 175

Maiden Form Brassiere Company, 136, 139

make-up mirror, 143–144, 150

Makin' Bacon cooker, 180–181

Managing Martians (Shirley and Morton), 155–156

Mangano, Joy, 47–49

Manhattan Project, 84, 189–190

Manning, Ann Harned, 3, 5, 191

marble, cultured, 30

Maric, Mileva, 190

Marion, Laura, 175

Markam, Lucille, 131

Mars rover, 153–156

Martian rock discovery, 161

Marwood, 127–128

Masters, Sybilla, 1, 5, 115

"Math Blaster" software, 83

mathematical ecology, 118

Mattel, 170, 171

Maxwell, Nicole, 124–126

McClintock, Barbara, 109

McClintock, Martha K., 114

McNulty, Kathleen, 84

McQueary, Agnes, 42–43

mechanical devices, 19–20,
  26–29
Meitner, Lise, 189
Melitta system, 40
"memory alloy," 167
Menton, Maude, 109
Merck Pharmaceuticals, 95, 96
Metcalf, Betsy, 194
Michaelis, Leonor, 109
"microbicide," 113–114
microelectronics chip design,
  81–82
microprocessors, 16–18
milking machine, 34
Miller, Darlene, 176
Miller, Hinda, 139–140
Miracle Mop, 47–49
Mitchell, Janet, 35
Mitterand, François, on Marie
  Curie, 195
"Mixed-Up Mother Goose"
  computer game, 65
molecular filters, 128
Money Talks bill reader,
  181–182
Montagu, Mary, 89
Morgan, Isabel, 113
Morgan, Lilian Vaughan,
  112–113
"morphing," 70
Morton, Danelle, 155
motel, automated, 29
Mothers of Invention (Vare and
  Ptacek), 1, 2, 3, 176
Motion Study (Gilbreth and
  Gilbreth), 54–55
motor, electric, 28
Moussa, Farag, 2

Muller, Gertrude, 133
Murphy, Patricia D., 114
"Mystery House" computer
  game, 65

N
NASA
  Deep Space 2 probes, 166
  Discovery space shuttle, 157
  Hypervelocity Impact Shield,
    167
  Lyndon B. Johnson Space
    Center, 156
  Mars rover, 153–156
  Research Center, 162
  Rogallo Wing, 172–173
  space suit, 158, 159
Natali, Susan, 144
National Hardware Men's
  Association, 42
National Inventive Thinking
  Association, 178
National Inventors Hall of Fame,
  2, 8, 47
National Medal of Technology,
  63
Nearly Me breast prothesis, 150,
  171–172
needle threader, 58
Nesmith, Michael, 13, 14, 15
network debugging system,
  74–75
"neural network" speech
  recognition program,
  185–186
Nightengale, Florence, 112
Norvir, 96
Notarandrea, Giovanna, 131

Nusselein-Volhard, Christiane, 195
nystatin, 97–99

O

o.b. tampon, 144–145
Ochoa, Ellen, 156–158
office products, 13–15, 31–32
oil filter, nonpolluting marine, 126–127
oil spill cleanup, 131
O'Leary, Lydia, 150
Olson, Sheri J., 114
Omerod, Eleanor, 116
O'Neill, Rose, 169
open-heart surgery, 191
optical imaging, 156–158
Osterholm, Jewell L., 114

P

packing peanuts, 123
Page, Alicia, 74
Pall, Teri, 3, 21–23
Pallas Athena, 5
Palo Alto Research Center, 81
paper bag, 26–28
Parkhurst, Carmemina, 29
Parpart, Florence, 6
patents
    description of, 201
    items covered by, 159, 202
    need for, 202
    obtaining, 202–204
Patrick, Ruth, 116
Paulsen, Twila, 131
peanut brittle, 57
Pearce, Louise, 90

Pennica, Diane, 107–109
Pennington, Mary Engle, 20–21, 38
Pepperidge Farm, 57
Perkins, Nancy, 34
Perlman, Katherine, 169
permanent waving machine, 147–149
Personal Communicator, 31–32
Pet Restrainer for Car Safety, 34
Petrini, Grace, 58
"Phantasmagoria" computer game, 66
pheromones, 114
Philadelphia Clinical Laboratory, 21
Phillips, Elizabeth, 175
Phillips, Tracy, 181–182
phone, cordless, 21–23
phone, disposable, 32–33
Pinckney, Elizabeth Lucas, 115
Pinkham, Lydia, 90
pizza, frozen, 51–52
planets, discovery of, 163, 164–165
Pocket Diaper, 186–187
pollutant scanner, 129–130
Poole, Olivia, 43
Popescu, Elena, 58
potato chips in bags, 44–45
Potts, Mary, 38
protease inhibitors, 93, 95–97
protecting invention, 203–204
Provisional Patent Application, 204
pulsar, 160
Purinethol, 92
Purple Moon, 82

Push Cush, 113
Putre, Mary, 174

Q
Quimby, Harriet, 152

R
radioimmunoassay, 99–100
Raphael, Sally, 47
reaper, 191
Recycle Design, 127
Redactron, 73
refrigeration, 21
refrigerator design, 55, 57–58
Revenge toilet paper, 174
Revson, Rommy, 140–141
Richards, Ellen Swallow, 116
Richardson, Josephine, 6
Rideout, Janet, 3, 4, 93–94
Ritter, Gladys, 133
Robinson, Laura, 175
Rodgers, Dorothy, 38
Roebling, Washington Augustus
    and Emily Warren, 192
Rogallo, Gertrude and Francis,
    172–173
Rolf, Ida, 103–104
Rose, Hilary, 2
Rosenthal, Ida Cohen, 136, 139
Rozier, Betty, 113
Rudkin, Margaret, 57
Russell, Alexander Wilson, 61
Russell, Inge, 128–129
Ryan, Catherine, 34
Ryan, Pamela, 173

S
Sabin, Florence, 91, 112

Safe-T Man, 150
safety-needle devices, 113
Samelson, Judy A., 127
Schlotter, Ann, 175
Schroeder, Becky, 183–184
scientific method, 22
Score, Roberta, 160–161
Scotchgard, 46–47
Scudder, Laura, 44–45
Scunci, 140–141
Se Ling-she, 5
Semiramis, Queen, 5
sewing machine, automatic,
    53–54
Shelby, Helene, 176
Sherman, Patsy, 46–47
Shipley, Mrs., 113
Shirley, Donna, 151, 153–156,
    194
Shotwell, Odette, 122–123,
    124
Siems, Ruth, 50–51
Sierra On-Line, 64, 65, 66
signal flare, maritime, 23–25
Singer, Isaac, 53
Skewes, Susan, 113
skyscraper construction, 191
Slater, Hannah, 1, 201
Sloane, Bill, 124
Slocum, Mary, 175
SMARTS, 75
Snyder, Betty, 84, 86
softball helmet for girls, 173
software
    computer games, 63–66, 174
    eco-software, 118–119
    Face Software, 70, 71
    "Math Blaster," 83

Sojourner Truth Mars rover, 151, 153–156
Somerville, Mary, 67
space discoveries, 160–166
space suit, 158–159
Spic and Span, 52
Stanley, Autumn, 2, 53
Stern, Kathleen, 114
Stevens, Nettie M., 191
Stiles, Elizabeth, 6
Stovall, Lisa, 184–185
Stove Top Stuffing, 50–51
Strong, Harriet, 58
Stuart, Miranda, 111–112
Stuckey, Joan, 113
Summer, Susan Kasen, 76, 77
supercomputer, 80
Super Slurper, 122, 123–124
superyeast, 128–129
surgery, 101–102, 104–107, 191
Swanson, Gloria, 58
Swanson & Sons, 50
System Management Arts, 75

T
Tacke, Ida Eva, 189
Tane, Victoria, 150
Taussig, Helen, 90–91
telephones, 21–23, 32–33, 78
telomerase, 109–111
Tereby, Susan, 164–165
Tesoro, Giuliana, 58
Thaden, Louise, 152
Thalidomide, 18
Thermagon, 82
Thompson, Teresa and Mary, 183–184
3-D innovations, 76–77

3-D Technology Laboratory, 77
Thunder TeePee, 73
Thurber, Denise Schelter, 114
Tick and Small Crawling Creature Barrier, 34
Tiller Turtle, 131
timeline of invention, 197–200
Todd, Lori A., 129–130
Toidy Seat, 133
Toole, Betty, 67
Topsy Tail, 141–142
Totino, Rose, 51–52
t-PA, 107–109
tract housing, 25–26
transsexuality, 79–80, 82
trash container, step-on, 54–55
Trotula, 111
Truth, Sojourner, 151
Tuska, C. D., 2
TV dinners, 50
typewriter, electric, 14

U
Universal Automatic Computer (UNIVAC), 86
urinalysis, 100
U.S. Department of Agriculture, 120–121, 122–123
U.S. Department of Labor Women's Bureau, 6, 37
U.S. Navy, 61
U.S. Patent and Trademark Office, 204, 206
U.S. Women's Pure Food Vacuum Preserving Company, 20
USS *Hopper*, 63

V

vacuum canning, 20–21
Vacuum Dirt Mat, 188
Valer, Johaan, 13
Vallino, Lisa, 113
Vassileva, Blagina, 113
Very, E. W., 23
very large-scale integrated
    circuits (VLSI), 81
Villaruz, Magdalena, 131
Villella, Jamie Lynn, 177, 188
virtual film set, 68–69
Visivox, 29–30
voice-controlled devices,
    16–18
voice monitor, 29–30
voting machine, 34

W

Wait, Mary, 57
Wakefield, Ruth, 38
Walker, Sarah Breedlove
    ("Madam C. J."), 145–147,
    148, 149
Walton, Mary, 5–6, 116
wash-and-wear fabrics, 58
washing machine design, 55,
    57–58
Watson, James, 110
Weaver, Mary Ollidene, 122,
    123–124
Web site resources, 205–207
welding, 35
Wellness Checkpoint, 83
Wells, Jane, 43
Wescoff, Marlyn, 84

Whitney, Eli, 10–11, 194
Williams, Roberta, 59, 63–66
windshield wiper, 19–20
Witch Doctor's Apprentice
    (Maxwell), 124
witches, burning of, 89–90
Women's Bureau (Department
    of Labor), 6, 37
Wonderful Hair Grower,
    145–147
workstation for handicapped,
    74
Wright, Katharine, 152
Wristies, 182–183
Wu, Chien-Shiung, 190

X

xanthan gum, 119–121
X-1 project, 158

Y

Yalow, Rosalyn Sussman,
    99–100
Yeager, Chuck, 158
Yemini, Shaula Alexander,
    74–75
Young, William G., 57

Z

Zeng, Bin, 114
zeolite Y, 128
Zhao, Chen, 3, 93, 95, 96–97
zigzag sewing machine, 53
Zimmerman, Rachel, 75–76
Zucker, JoAnn, 6
Zyloprim, 92